A Biblical Journey Through The Irish Year

With True Stories, Reflections & Photographs

o-o-o-o-o

To my parents, Jack & Ella Hutchinson.

o-o-o-o-o

"My heart is inditing a good matter: I speak of the things which I have made touching the King: my tongue is the pen of a ready writer."
(Psalm 45v1)

By Elizabeth Burke

Acknowledgements

I wish to express my gratitude to Ms. Anne-Marie Diffley in Trinity College, Dublin, for permission to photograph the "Long Room," and to Ms. Annetta Flanigan, whose name was mentioned with her permission, in "Wars, Rumours of War, Three Hostages – and the Prayers of the Saints." Many thanks to my mother, Ella Hutchinson and my daughter, Sarah Hutchinson Burke, for the inspiration of their lovely artwork which complement chapters 2 and 23.

(Cover Photograph – Scenery near Stradbally in Co. Laois)

Published by:
Mrs. Elizabeth Burke,
Ready Writer Publications,
Saddlestown,
Stamullen,
Co. Meath,
Republic of Ireland.

ISBN: 978-0-9557155-0-1

Contents

Introduction

There is something about living in the Irish rolling countryside that inspires one to write! Every facet of life, from my walks in lonely lanes and glens - to old memories, experiences and observations of my fellow human travellers, offers an abundance of material to draw from.

The following twenty-four chapters are based on true stories and experiences. Consisting of parables, reflections and object lessons, they touch on the Trinity, the brevity of life, the occult, education, love, death, illness, forgiveness, God's provisions, the all-atoning sacrifice of Jesus, Hell, Heaven, prayer and the need for salvation amongst other issues. I wish to thank the Lord for showing me that behind each experience throughout a year lies a treasure trove of spiritual lessons to be learned, and that the Bible has something to say about every experience and occasion, including the traditional seasons with which we are all accustomed. Above all it is my sincere desire that He would be glorified in the pages that follow; that those who know Him would be blessed, encouraged or challenged – while those who have 'backslidden' or not yet trusted the Saviour, would be alerted to the danger of life without Christ, both in this life and the next.

At "The Gate of the Year"
(Psalm 90v12)

(January 1st - January 15th)

In many a dusty attic lie the private daily memories of individuals, recorded in books called diaries. Not so long ago, my children in their exploration of our attic, found old diaries belonging to me, some of which were recorded when I was even younger than they are today. They shrieked with laughter when they read them, because of course, times have changed. But I had a far away look in my eyes when they were reading and laughing. How the years had changed me! It was almost as if a different person had written the words, and yet, it is true, that some of the memories returned to me. I remembered the vulnerable, often sensitive child that I had been, and how life had seemed difficult on occasions. Nevertheless, when I return to those scenes of childhood – how beautiful they were!

I met someone once whose childhood memories were not so happy. Her diaries, if she'd had the opportunity to write any, would have read very differently to mine. Sadly she was flung into an institution at an early age because of home circumstances. One of her earliest memories is of being mercilessly beaten and abused in her new, terrifying 'home.' Our experiences in life can very often change and shape our personalities over the years. A smell, a taste, a voice, a sound, an object, an old photograph, or some words in a diary - can ignite the flames of poignant memories, which touch the human soul, and bring a tear to the eye. Some people may grow bitter and feel alienated by unhappy times in their lives, but if we have given our lives unreservedly to the Lord, He has promised to heal our broken hearts and use even the memory of those negative experiences to bring us close to Him, our Rock, and Fortress. (Psalm 18v2) In Psalm 90v9 we read... "For all our days are passed away in thy wrath: we spend our years as a tale that is told."

"We spend our years as a tale that is told..." How true is that phrase! One has only to read the day to day records of an old diary, to see the true story of a life unfolding. Behind the short phrases in my diaries lies a world of painful and happy memories, known only to myself, and to those who shared the experiences. Looking through an old diary, I can see that page after page describes the mundane, joyful or unhappy events of a year in my life. The fourth verse of that lovely old hymn: 'I know whom I have believed,' by El Nathan, could well be used to summarise the veiled days that lie ahead for the Christian…

"I know not what of good or ill
May be reserved for me,
Of weary ways or golden days
Before His face I see…"

As I embark upon my journey on the unknown paths of another year, I am often reminded of an extract from a poem entitled 'God Knows,' by Minnie Louise Haskins (1875-1957). These (now famous) words were used by King George VI in his Christmas address to the British nation, shortly after the outbreak of the Second World War in 1939…

"And I said to the man who stood at the gate of the year,
Give me a light
That I may tread safely into the unknown.
And he replied
Go out into the darkness
And put your hand into the Hand of God
That shall be to you
Better than light
And safer than a known way."

This destructive war was to be the worst that Europe had ever known, radical political changes would take place, and borders would ultimately be redrawn – many never to be the same again. Over fifty million people died, amongst them around six million Jews - the Lord's ancient chosen people. To step out into any unknown fierce battle or into any dark tomorrow, surely as the poem rightly says - the only safe thing to do is to place our hand in that of the Saviour's. In our lives, the known, the conventional and even the 'well-lit' route, may not always turn out as expected, but if our "times are in His hand," (Psalm 31v15), we may walk confidently into the 'darkest abyss,' that life throws at us.

Years ago my family and I visited a unique old dwelling and out buildings in a quiet rural location. The resident family appeared industrious and full of the joys of life. I remember buying some of their produce on that summer's day. Then, years later one of my daughters asked me to return there with her, as she had remembered the location and wanted to use the scene for an art project. Driving up the narrow lane on an early misty winter's morning, I could scarcely believe that this was the same place. Staring over the steering wheel, I knitted my eyebrows. *Was* this the place, or were we lost? Even the signpost had become partially hidden by years of growth. Cobwebs covered the windows, ivy and weeds clung to the walls, the pond was stagnant and the wheel of the mill no longer turned. "This place scares me. Let's get out of here," whispered my daughter. I knew what she meant. There was a strange eerie atmosphere on that still, frosty winter morning, as our breath rose in little clouds. I knocked on the old heavy door of the grey house, somehow not expecting an answer. However, in response to my knock I heard footsteps within, drawing closer and closer. My daughter clutched my arm.

The man who stood there, it appeared to me, bore no resemblance to the younger man whom we had met years previously. He looked much older, grey, tired and had grown a moustache. I told him of our errand that morning, and he smilingly assured us that we could take the necessary photographs. As he disappeared through the great door again, I turned to my daughter. "Surely that isn't the same man?" I asked.

"Of course it is Mum. I remember him," she replied, "but something has changed him…" I nodded. She has always been more observant than I. "Perhaps life has been hard on him…" We walked towards the old mill wheel, which lay motionless and choked with weeds that grey winter morning. 'Such a pity,' I thought, as we took the photographs, 'after years of work…'

"Let's go, Mum. This place gives me the creeps. I feel like we're in a time warp. Maybe that was a ghost we were talking to!"

"Of course not," I laughed, as we drove back up the overgrown narrow lane, leaving a scene revisited, "but wasn't everything so strangely different from the last time?"

After several years it was evident that dramatic changes had taken place in the lives of those who once lived there. Indeed, any period of time can bring about radical changes in our own lives. It is true to say that a mere split second can result in a terrible accident that could change one's life forever. Nevertheless, in the changing scenes of time, it is important to remember two things. Firstly, our loving Saviour *never* changes... "Jesus Christ the same yesterday, and to day and for ever" – (Hebrews 13v8). Our 'nearest and dearest' upon this earth may fail us, but "He faileth not," (Zephaniah 3v5). Secondly, how are our Christian lives? Has the joy gone, or like the old millpond – have we become dangerously choked by the 'weeds' of this world? Always remember that He who "changeth not" will not despise "a broken and a contrite heart." (Psalm 51v17)

For the Christian, the unknown should not be a frightening prospect – but a challenging one. We must, in the powerful words of Ephesians 6v11, "Put on the whole armour of God, that ye may be able to stand against the wiles of the devil." Like those soldiers who went out to battle in the Second World War, we must be fully equipped. "Wherefore take unto you the whole armour of God, that ye may be able to withstand in the evil day, and having done all, to stand." (V13) But our armour, as we advance into spiritual warfare, is not of this world, as we learn in Verses 14-18: "Stand therefore, having your loins girt about with truth, and having on the breastplate of righteousness; And your feet shod with the preparation of the gospel of peace; Above all, taking the shield of faith, wherewith ye shall be able to quench all the fiery darts of the wicked. And take the helmet of salvation, and the sword of the Spirit, which is the word of God: Praying always with all prayer and supplication in the Spirit, and watching thereunto with all perseverance and supplication for all saints;" Let us remember, as we walk closely with Him, that "the battle is the Lord's," and "He saveth not with sword or spear." (1Sam. 17v47). For those who are not walking with Him.... Repent of all that previous life, outside of His grace, put your hand into His today, and trust Him with all your tomorrows!

Few of us need to be reminded that life is transient. In Psalm 90v10-11 we read: "The days of our years are threescore years and ten; and if by reason of strength they be fourscore years, yet is their strength labour and sorrow; for it is soon cut off, and we fly away. Who knoweth the power of thine anger? Even according to thy fear, so is thy wrath."

Whatever our profession of faith or lack of it, judgement is inevitable for all of us... "So then every one of us shall give account of himself to God." (Romans 14v12). Again in 1Pet. 4v17&18 we read... "For the time is come that judgement must begin at the house of God: and if it first begin at us, what shall the end be of them that obey not the gospel of God? And if the righteous scarcely be saved, where shall the ungodly and sinner appear?" For all of us, this could be the year of the Lord's return – or for some of us, it could be our last year as individuals. Oh that we would ensure that we are ready for that Day, so that an eternity of golden days (happier than we have known upon this earth) may be ours! "So teach us to number our days, that we may apply our hearts unto wisdom. Return, O lord, how long? And let it repent thee concerning thy servants. O satisfy us early with thy mercy; that we may rejoice and be glad all our days. Make us glad according to the days wherein thou hast afflicted us, and the years wherein we have seen evil. Let thy work appear unto thy servants, and thy glory unto their children. And let the beauty of the Lord our God be upon us; yea, the work of our hands establish thou it." (Psalm 90v12-17)

I cannot know the future,
No more than change the past,
But on Jesus Christ my Saviour –
My every care I'll cast.

(Job 23v10)

Gates leading to a country laneway, near Woodview, Armagh.

(2)

Looks Promising!
(1John 2v15-17 & 1John 2v25)

(January 16th - January 31st)

Great jewels of icy rain ran down the kitchen window pane, as I stared pensively at the shadowy fields beyond our own. A black cloud of crows were flying towards the trees of the glen, and as darkness began to fall the last birds of dusk sang for yet another little while. 'At least the days are getting slightly longer,' I thought as I hastily transferred the vegetables to the stove. The winter's day had been a typically Irish one... stark trees bent to a blustery wind, and clouds that were continually bursting with cold rain or sleet. As steam started to rise from the pot of Irish stew, I heard a thud from the hall letterbox. "Anything interesting in the post?" I shouted to my daughter who was gathering it from the floor.
"Just junk mail really... oh, here's a nice colourful brochure." Taking it from her, I quickly flicked through it with a smile. The glossy cover read: 'Book before 31st January and get 25% off this year's summer holiday - hurry now!'
Glancing outdoors at the dark wintry scene, and then back to the brochure, I was instantly transported to an exotic paradise of azure blue skies and seas, golden sands fringed with palm trees and endless sunshine. 'Looks wonderful,' I thought, 'but what about the prices?' Opening a separate enclosed leaflet, my heart sank. Huh, we could forget about those particular destinations. What a rip-off - even *with* the 25% discount! Anyway, there were more practical considerations at the moment... 'Still though,' I thought wistfully, 'it was exciting to explore new places...' My thoughts returned to an older glossy brochure, from decades ago, and my subsequent journey to the city of Istanbul, where Europe and Asia converge. The 'accommodation' had been beautifully portrayed on the glossy page, but reality was quite another story! Quickly my thoughts flew through the years, and I chuckled when I thought about some of the glossy brochures - and then the stark reality of each trip, in turn. Thankfully, there had been no *real* horror stories, and some of them

had actually been enjoyable - but those glossy pages rarely live up to our expectations!

Many years later, and much closer to home, my husband and I decided to take a couple of days away to celebrate our wedding anniversary. Before the break I had lingered over our destination in anticipation. The guesthouse appeared to be set amongst trees: in sylvan surroundings, yet near the coast. It looked truly idyllic. Eventually, when we found the place it turned out to be on a busy main road! Inviting us in to the shabby old period house, the owner quickly closed over a door, when he saw that I was about to look in. "Oh you wouldn't want to see in there just now," he said clearing his throat, "something's just happened to the dining room ceiling..." They had a swimming pool on the premises, which was one of the things that had attracted my husband, but all too soon we discovered that this pool was very ancient, unhygienic, and none of the other guests used it!

Now on a wintry afternoon in my warm kitchen, I thoughtfully turned my attention from that glossy brochure to a little 'box of promises,' which had been sitting on the windowsill for many years. Shaped like a small loaf of bread, inscribed upon it were the words: "Bread of Life." Dropping the brochure, I walked over to it and picked out one of its comforting promises... "Him that overcometh will I make a pillar in the temple of my God..." (Rev. 3v12). "Him that overcometh..." 'Yes,' I thought, 'there is so much to overcome in this world, but if we have put our trust in the power of the risen Saviour - then we may overcome *by faith.*' "For whatsoever is born of God overcometh the world: and this is the victory that overcometh the world, even our faith. Who is he that overcometh the world, but he that believeth that Jesus is the Son of God?" (1John 5v4&5).

No sooner is the festive season over, than we are inundated by advertising and special offers from many sources. "Avail of our new 'body sculpting' package at Jennifer's Gym," or "end the winter blues with a facial at Barbara's Beauty Clinic." So many in this world rush on, enthralled with the passing pleasures of life - but afraid of death.

Never in the recorded history of mankind have there been so many people requiring unnecessary surgery to change everything from their features - to their gender. Many strive for the temporal, caring nothing for the spiritual, the unseen - the promise of eternal life to those whose delight is in the Lord. Surely "our sufficiency is of God" (2Cor. 3v5), and "He satisfieth the longing soul, and filleth the hungry soul with goodness." (Psalm 107v9). Many are afraid of the 'ageing process,' and would go to any lengths to postpone it. Not only the rich and famous suffer the pain of this type of surgery - and the end results are very often less than desirable! If only they could see the wisdom of that lovely verse... "The glory of young men is their strength: and the beauty of old men is the gray head." (Prov. 20v29).

Eternal youth, idyllic holidays, a beautiful physique, flawless skin - we are promised so much in that glossy junk mail which preys on those suffering from low spirits and 'post-Christmas blues.' "Vanity of vanities, saith the preacher; all is vanity." (Eccl. 12v8). Surely, none but Christ can satisfy! Psalm 1 proclaims the mark of the Christian... "But his delight is in the law of the Lord; and in his law doth he meditate day and night. And he shall be like a tree planted by the rivers of water, that bringeth forth his fruit in his season; his leaf also shall not wither; and whatsoever he doeth shall prosper." (Verses 2&3).

In 1John 2v15-17 we are exhorted... "Love not the world, neither the things that are in the world. If any man love the world, the love of the Father is not in him. For all that is in the world, the lust of the flesh, and the lust of the eyes, and the pride of life, is not of the Father, but is of the world. And the world passeth away, and the lust thereof: but he that doeth the will of God abideth for ever." The world with all its illusions and empty promises! Unlike the words on some glossy brochure, God's promises to man (of which there are over 7,000) are unfailing. The Bible does not try to sell us some trouble-free experience. "In the world ye shall have tribulation: but be of good cheer; I have overcome the world," Jesus promises us in John 16v33. If we have trusted Him as Saviour, then we are "heirs according to the promise," as portrayed in Rom. 9v7&8, and Gal. 3v29.

One by one, I took out my little promises and read them... "In the day of trouble I will call upon thee: for thou wilt answer me." (Psalm 86v7). "When thou passeth through the waters, I will be with thee." (Isaiah 43v2). "Thou wilt keep him in perfect peace whose mind is stayed on thee." (Isaiah 26v3). Such reassuring promises, and what warm memories I had of the comfort they had brought me in uncertain times! I remember one troubled dark night reading… "Many are the afflictions of the righteous: but the Lord delivereth him out of them all." (Psalm 34v19). Of course they are no substitute for reading the Bible, and studying whole passages in their entirety, but I believe that the Lord can often use them to bring encouragement in all types of situations.

Behind each one of God's promises, however, lies a condition. These conditions could well be summarised in the words of Jesus: "If ye abide in me, and my words abide in you, ye shall ask what ye will, and it shall be done unto you." (John 15v7). To the Christian He says: "Let that therefore abide in you, which ye have heard from the beginning. If that which ye have heard from the beginning shall remain in you, ye shall also continue in the Son, and in the Father. And this is the promise He hath promised us, even eternal life." (1John 2v24&25). And to a world of lost souls for whom His precious blood was shed, He promises: "I am the bread of life: he that cometh to me shall never hunger; and he that believeth on me shall never thirst." (John 6v35). …"Whereby are given unto us exceeding great and precious promises: that by these ye might be partakers of the divine nature, having escaped the corruption that is in the world through lust…" (2Pet. 1v4). Oh that all, through faith, would obtain these great and marvellous promises!

This world offers nothing but the passing,
Earthly disappointments, that which causes strife,
*But **His** promises are sure and everlasting,*
Never broken in the changing scenes of life.

"Primroses and Promises" – *A painting by Sarah Hutchinson Burke.*

The Greatest Gift
(1Cor. 13v13)

(February 1st- February 14th)

The back door of our little country bungalow creaked open as usual that dark Friday evening. However, instead of greeting one person (my husband upon his usual return from work) now I was greeting two! His brother, whom I had not seen for almost two decades, stood there beside him looking awkward, hesitant. I greeted him with spontaneous warmth, telling him how wonderful it was to see him after all these years. Exchanging glances, I knew that he was thinking about how much I had changed - and I had the same thoughts about him! The rigours of life had surely left their mark on all of us. We sat down to dinner, and soon he was meeting my three daughters, two of them for the very first time. My eldest daughter was a baby when he had left the country all those years ago. They had never known him and were intrigued with this 'long lost uncle,' as we had affectionately named him over the years.

We had located him some time previously, with my husband's parents' approaching 50th wedding anniversary in mind. They had not seen him in many years and how wonderful, I felt, would be the surprise re-union, if only they could possibly meet again. Now that re-union was imminent and I was looking forward to the surprise party which had been prepared for them the following day. Meanwhile, he would stay at our house and next day we would bring him to his old home.

The special afternoon in question arrived all too soon. Another brother-in-law had arranged for the 'anniversary couple' to be elsewhere, while we all gathered into the family home. Soon the caterers arrived with some tasty delicacies, and 'the long lost uncle' was hiding in the garden shed until after the arrival of my parents-in-law. It was planned that we would call him on his mobile, at the moment when he was required to make the 'grand entrance!' Meanwhile, the doorbell rang and a beautiful bouquet of flowers arrived from my mother-in-law's sister. At that point someone came up with the bright idea of giving the flowers to 'the long lost uncle', and suggested that he (initially) pretend to be the flower deliveryman.

I felt emotional as my parents-in-law arrived for their party. There were joyful greetings and jubilant congratulations, as the little living room filled with happy voices. Numerous telephone calls followed, some neighbours called in person to congratulate them and then the door bell rang... My father-in-law went out into the hallway first, there was complete silence for a moment, and then I heard his voice choking out his son's name with surprised emotion "_____!" My eyes too, filled with tears as my brother-in-law entered the hallway and hugged his parents. At this point, I could not help but think of other joyous reunions - that of the prodigal son and his father, which is recounted in Luke 15v11-32; and when Joseph was reunited with his brothers, and subsequently his father, in Genesis 46v29. Although they had not met in a very long time, here was that love displayed between them! The intervening years had made no difference to the love of parents towards their offspring and the love of a son for his mother and father. "Many waters cannot quench love, neither can the floods drown it: if a man would give all the substance of his house for love, it would utterly be contemned." (Song of Solomon 8v7).

How wonderful, too, was the fact that, after fifty years of marriage, this couple was still together and happy to be in each other's company! Swans, I have learned, also keep the same lifetime partner - which is why they are often depicted on wedding anniversary cards, as a symbol of fidelity. However, where the human race is concerned, nowadays the very institution of marriage itself is under threat. Sadly, many people move from 'partner to partner' with an alarming disregard for the Word of God. On Valentine's Day we hear much talk about 'romantic love,' but the love which grows between a couple who have been together for as long as my parents, or my husband's parents, is anything but superficial. Through the years it has been tested and tried in the furnace of disappointments, illnesses and the death of loved ones... Real love, the intense love that "suffereth long, and is kind" (1Cor. 13v4), is very rare in today's world.

As my brother-in-law sat there beside his parents, I felt that it was a very private and poignant moment for all of them. I thought of my own relationship with my children and how much I loved them. It would be a rare and incongruous matter indeed, if a mother abandoned her children, and yet I have read and heard of situations where this has happened. Hence we read in Isaiah 49v15: "Can a woman forget her suckling child, that she should not have compassion on the son of her womb? Yea, they may forget, yet will I not forget thee." A mother's love is used in this analogy because it is one of the most unselfish and self-sacrificing. Many mothers would give their very lives for their children. However, even a mother may fail to love her offspring, but God's love towards each one of us is perfect - and transcends all loves!

In 1John 4v10 we read: "Herein is love, not that we loved God, but that he loved us, and sent his Son to be the propitiation for our sins." God, in fact *is love*, as we learn in both verses 8 and 16 of this chapter. In 1John 4v11 we are commanded... "Beloved, if God so loved us, we ought also to love one another." Obviously, John is exhorting Christians here. Only those who have been truly born again of the Spirit of God have the love of God shed abroad in their hearts (Rom. 5v5), enabling them to love others as they should. It is His will that *all* should know Him, and that those who *have* given their lives to Him, should love their 'brethren in the Lord.' In 1John 4v12 we read: "No man hath seen God at any time. If we love one another, God dwelleth in us, and his love is perfected in us." Also, if our first love is the Author of all love, then surely we will have that love in our hearts for all souls, whatever their spiritual standing, just as Jesus did when He walked upon this earth?

Prior to that memorable weekend, I had only met my husband's brother two or three times and yet God had put a love for his soul within my heart. I had often prayed for him, not knowing his situation or whereabouts - but God knew! "Hereby know we that we dwell in him, and he in us, because he hath given us of his Spirit." (1John 4v13). I am sure that he would have been more comfortable staying in a 'five star' hotel, than our cramped little bungalow. However, the hotel may have been cold, impersonal, far from homely - and very expensive! In contrast to this he was staying with people who genuinely cared about his welfare and who did not want anything in return. In Proverbs 15v17 we read: "Better is a dinner of herbs where love is, than a stalled ox and hatred therewith."

Just over a year later, on February 14th (traditionally known as Valentine's Day), I happened to be in a local town with my daughters who were on a mid-term break, when by chance I met a couple whom I had not seen in a very long time. I was aware that they had, at one time, been connected with a local Christian fellowship. However, something had happened (which I had no knowledge of) and this couple were now estranged from that particular fellowship. My immediate reaction was to cordially greet the couple and their little children. If it had been otherwise, I would seriously have had to question my very relationship with the Saviour. "And we have known and believed the love that God hath to us. God is love; and he that dwelleth in love dwelleth in God, and God in him. Herein is our love made perfect, that we may have boldness in the day of judgement: because as he is, so are we in this world." (1John 4v16&17).

Within Christian circles there may arise many issues which cause dissension - not just doctrinal ones. However, nothing should alter our love for our brothers and sisters in Christ; for we read... "We know that we have passed from death unto life, because we love the brethren. He that loveth not his brother abideth in death. Whosoever hateth his brother is a murderer: and ye know that no murderer hath eternal life abiding in him. Hereby perceive we the love of God, because he laid down his life for us: and we ought to lay down our lives for the brethren." (1John 3v14-16). In situations where, because of sin, a person is no longer in Christian fellowship, those "which are spiritual" are exhorted to "restore such an one in the spirit of meekness, considering thyself, lest thou also be tempted." (Gal.6v1). It is a terrible situation where people would look the other way, or even cross the street, in preference to greeting someone whom they would once have acknowledged was a brother or sister in Christ. If our greeting is ignored, the Lord will assist us to continue praying for the person (or people) concerned. And so we read in 1John 4v20&21: "If a man say, I love God, and hateth his brother, he is a liar: for he that loveth not his brother whom he hath seen, how can he love God whom he hath not seen? And this commandment have we from him, That he who loveth God loveth his brother also."

Scattered throughout the world, there is a precious band of believers, who are collectively known as "the body of Christ." (1Cor. 12v27). Of differing nations, cultures, classes and gender - each day is a walk of faith for them. Jesus says of His relationship with them: "I am the good Shepherd, and know my sheep, and am known of mine." (John 10v14). We also learn that each one who names the name of Christ, has been endowed with differing spiritual gifts. "Now there are diversities of gifts, but the same Spirit. And there are differences of administrations, but the same Lord. And there are diversities of operations, but it is the same God which worketh all in all. But the manifestation of the Spirit is given to every man to profit withal." (1Cor. 12v4-7). "For the body is not one member, but many." (1Cor.12v14).

Just as the human body (we learn in 1Cor. 12v15-17) contains many essential members which contribute to its successful life, so too, does that spiritual body, "the body of Christ." In 1Cor. 12v28-30 we read: "And God hath set some in the church, first apostles, secondarily prophets, thirdly teachers, after that miracles, then gifts of healings, helps, governments, diversities of tongues. Are all apostles? Are all prophets? Are all teachers? Are all workers of miracles? Have all the gifts of healing? Do all speak with tongues? Do all interpret?" Finally, in verse 31 of this chapter, we are exhorted to... "Covet earnestly the best gifts: and yet shew I unto you a more excellent way."

It is possible for a Pastor (or any Christian) to be very knowledgeable in sound doctrine; to know his Bible 'inside-out,' believing every word therein and have 'mountain moving faith' - but to be lacking in love! Imagine a situation where someone stumbles to that Christian's door one night. He has been involved in a car accident, there is blood dripping everywhere, glass in his hair and he is suffering from shock. Outside the night is cold and damp but the 'Christian' insists that the injured party sit outdoors on his garden seat. "I can't let his blood drip all over my new carpet," he mutters, while telephoning for help. "This *would* have to happen, just as I was about to make my way to that meeting. No one there shares *my* expertise on the subject I was going to speak on this evening - and furthermore, I'm going to be late, if I get there at all!" Surely the following verse applies perfectly, in such a situation... "Though I speak with the tongues of men and of angels, and have not charity, I am become as sounding brass, or a tinkling cymbal." (1Cor. 13v1). It must be noted that this beautiful word *charity* was used in 17th century England, to describe love, in all its fullness.

I believe also, that as the love of God is limitless, so too is our potential for growth in this area. For the Christian, the beautiful gift of love in all its purity must be the motive behind our every endeavour. It is certainly true that 'actions speak louder than words.' My memories often return to that cold, dark evening when my brother-in-law stood there by the kitchen table, looking a little uncertain. I thank God that it was He who put that love in my heart, so that I could reach out to someone I now scarcely knew. The love of God had changed me. There was a time in my life when I would have put myself and my own convenience first, but "old things are passed away" (2Cor5v17).

"We love him, *because he first loved us.*" (1John 4v19) The love of God towards us is surely second to none. A husband may leave his wife; a wife may leave her husband; a mother may forget the child of her womb; a father may turn his back on his children; a son or daughter may turn away from parents; friends, brothers and sisters may revile us - *but God is love.* (1John 4v16). I once heard the true story of a young Jewish girl who had become a Christian. Her father told her: "as far as we are concerned, you are now *dead.*" Surely no one was more comforted by the following words, than that little girl ... "When my father and my mother forsake me, then the Lord will take me up." (Psalm 27v10). Jesus said: "Think not that I am come to send peace on earth: I am come not to send peace, but a sword. For I am come to set a man at variance against his father, and the daughter against her mother, and the daughter-in-law against her mother-in-law. And a man's foes shall be they of his own household. He that loveth father or mother more than me is not worthy of me: and he that loveth son or daughter more than me is not worthy of me." (Matt. 10v34-37).

Therefore, we learn that God, whose infinite love for us excels all loves, must be our *first* love; for "He that taketh not his cross, and followeth after me, is not worthy of me." (Matt. 10v38). When we put Him first in our lives, then He will put a love in our hearts for even the unlovely and those who revile us. He truly wants to be our closest Friend, above all others. We can trust Him with our deepest, most painful secrets. "There is a friend that sticketh closer than a brother," we learn in Proverbs 18v24. He wants, above all, to break the power of sin in our lives, so that we might not be "conformed to this world: ... but be ye transformed by the renewing of your mind, that ye may prove what is that good, and acceptable, and perfect, will of God." (Romans 12v2).

"Greater love hath no man than this," said Jesus, "that a man lay down his life for his friends." (John 15v13). Why not trust this Friend, whose love excels all loves? If you do so, He will want to shed His love abroad in your heart: "that perfect love which casteth out fear." (1 John 4v18). "For now we see through a glass darkly; but then face to face: now I know in part; but then shall I know even as also I am known. And now abideth faith, hope, charity, these three; but the greatest of these is charity." (1Cor. 13v12&13).

There is no greater gift than love,
Pure, undefiled, sent from above...
So ask thy Saviour to impart,
His gift of love to fill thy heart.

Swans at the lovely coastal village of Cushendun, Co. Antrim.

(4)

"Food for Thought…"
(Matt. 15v17-20)

(February 15th- February 29th)

"Armageddon for the Grocers! How Many More Timebombs in our Food Chain?" These alarming headlines stopped me in my tracks as I hurried into the supermarket. Glancing at my watch, I knew that I must quickly pick up something for dinner before driving the 13 miles to be at a certain place, at a certain time! As always that time was limited, so I threw the last copy of that worrying newspaper into my trolley, resolving to read it later. It was tempting, also, to throw in some convenience foods since life seemed to be such a rush these days, but today I must be careful!

I had been vaguely aware of this news some days ago but now I was concerned. Apparently a vast quantity of potentially dangerous convenience foods had escaped into the food chain. They had all been flavoured with imported Indian chilli which contained an illegal cancer-promoting dye, known as "Sudan 1." Alarmingly, the list of affected foods seemed to be growing by the day. The newspaper that I had picked up claimed to carry a fully up-dated list of the affected products. 'Is it any wonder that there is only one copy left?' I thought. 'People are naturally troubled about anything that may affect their health, their very lives.'

Looking around, it struck me how shopping had changed so much over the decades. My mother's £5 (sterling) once covered the cost of a week's shopping for herself, her husband and four children! Food, in many ways, was simpler and more wholesome in those days, I believe. The aroma of home-baked bread and scones, healthy soups and stews and fresh vegetables wafting from homesteads in the old days, are in stark contrast to today's pre-packed, microwaveable, additive-ridden 'quick meals.' Suspect meat has increased the number of vegetarians, and never have there been so many people with diverse food allergies. Quickly picking up a few necessities, I noticed the 'pancake mix' which had been reduced in the wake of 'Shrove Tuesday.' Like other products, it carried a list of 'E' numbers. "Well, at least I can make my own pancakes, with straightforward eggs, milk and flour," I muttered defensively. No, I wouldn't buy it, even at half price. It seemed nowadays that there was a 'mix' for everything, including life itself.

A few days later my youngest daughter came home from school with a pamphlet containing a list of 'recommended things to do, in our observance of Lent.' "Is it good to give up things for Lent Mum?" she asked. It was a good idea, I explained to her, to eat healthily, at *any* time of the year, and this may entail giving up or reducing our intake of sweets, for example. However, the Lord has never laid down any 'hard and fast' rules about eating things differently at certain times and seasons of the year. In 1Cor. 10v31 we are exhorted to "do all to the glory of God," which includes eating and drinking, but the word 'Lent' is nowhere to be found in the Bible.

Indeed, the whole idea that we can improve our spiritual standing before God by self denial of one sort or another, is totally contrary to God's Word, for we read in Titus 3v5-7: "Not by works of righteousness which we have done, but according to his mercy he saved us, by the washing of regeneration, and renewing of the Holy Ghost; Which he shed on us abundantly through Jesus Christ our Saviour; That being justified by his grace, we should be made heirs according to the hope of eternal life." Also, in 1Tim. 4v4 we read: "For every creature of God is good, and nothing to be refused, if it be received with thanksgiving: For it is sanctified by the word of God and prayer." It is interesting to note that *thanksgiving* is mentioned twice in this portion of scripture (1Tim. 4v1-5). How good (and essential) it is to give thanks for the food before us. This can be a challenge when one is dining in public - but we should never be ashamed to bow our heads and give thanks to the Lord for His provisions to us. This action in itself is a witness and testimony to those around us!

Many denominations now observe Lent as a 'holy time of preparation,' in the forty days prior to Easter. Preparation for what, I wonder, for surely the Great Ransom has been paid? (Heb. 10v10). No ordinance of man, or fasting, self-punishment or denial of certain foods and luxuries can take away the sin which separates us from God and from eternal life in His kingdom - but the blood of Jesus can! This Jesus "Who needeth not daily, as those high priests, to offer up sacrifice, first for his own sins, and then for the people's: for this he did once, when he offered up himself. For the law maketh men high priests which have infirmity; but the word of the oath, which was since the law, maketh the Son, who is consecrated for evermore." (Heb. 7v27&28).

Sadly many priests today, like the priests of old, find themselves subject to ordinances and laws which can never take away sin. Christians too, are warned... "Howbeit then, when ye knew not God, ye did service unto them which by nature are no gods. But now, after that ye have known God, or rather are known of God, how turn ye again to the weak and beggarly elements, whereunto ye desire again to be in bondage? Ye observe days, and months, and times, and years. I am afraid of you, lest I have bestowed upon you labour in vain." (Gal. 4v8-11).

Like the Pharisees of Bible days, many people these days live a seemingly 'holy' life, attending their place of worship regularly and adhering to directives from their hierarchy. Unlike the Christians of Berea, mentioned in Acts 17v10-13, they do not "search the scriptures daily, whether those things were so..." (v11). Surely we can only put our trust in "such an high priest... who is holy, harmless, undefiled, separate from sinners, and made higher than the heavens." (Heb. 7v26). Again, only Jesus can forgive us, cleanse us, and make us free from the indwelling sin, which every soul has been born with. In Matthew 15v11 He tells us... "Not that which goeth into the mouth defileth a man; but that which cometh out of the mouth, this defileth a man." At Peter's request, He gives a full explanation of this parable in verses 17-20... "Do not ye yet understand, that whatsoever entereth in at the mouth goeth into the belly, and is cast out into the draught? But those things which proceed out of the mouth come forth from the heart; and they defile the man. For out of the heart proceed evil thoughts, murders, adulteries, fornications, thefts, false witness, blasphemies: These are the things which defile a man: but to eat with unwashen hands defileth not a man."

The Jewish people (and Pharisees in particular) were very concerned about all the rituals and ordinances, regarding what they should or should not eat and how it should be eaten. What a revelation it must have been for Peter to see the vision of… "heaven opened, and a certain vessel descending unto him, as it had been a great sheet knit at the four corners, and let down to the earth: Wherein were all manner of fourfooted beasts of the earth, and wild beasts, and creeping things, and fowls of the air." (Acts 10v11&12).

In Luke chapter 10, we read those wise instructions that Jesus gave to His disciples, as He sent them forth to preach the gospel. Amongst these, in verses 7&8 we read: "And in the same house remain, eating and drinking such things as they give: for the labourer is worthy of his hire. Go not from house to house. And into whatsoever city ye enter, and they receive you, *eat such things as are set before you:*" There is no doubt that food differs tremendously throughout the nations of the world and to be a missionary perhaps one also needs to have a strong stomach! Years ago I recall speaking to a young Chinese man who informed me that portions of dog and cat were displayed in his native supermarkets! To the average Western mind the thought of eating domestic pets is inconceivable, and to eat rats (which are considered a delicacy in some societies) would be unwise, given that they carry disease! However, every situation in our lives as individuals and Christians, is different, and should be brought to the Lord in prayer. He will surely give us discernment for every decision we make, whether the issue is food and drink, or anything else in this life. Most of us will probably never find ourselves in a predicament where we are faced with having to eat rats, but should we do - the Lord will protect His own!

Therefore we learn that: "All things are lawful for me, but all things are not expedient: all things are lawful for me, but all things edify not." (1Cor. 10v23). The words of Paul echo the words of Jesus, for we read… "Whatsoever is sold in the shambles, that eat, asking no question for conscience sake: For the earth is the Lord's, and the fulness thereof. If any of them that believe not bid you to a feast, and ye be disposed to go; whatsoever is set before you, eat, asking no question for conscience sake." (1Cor. 10v25-27). The remainder of this chapter advises Christians *not* to eat or drink, when another's conscience, and therefore soul, is at stake. "Give none offence," we are told, "neither to the Jews, nor to the Gentiles, nor to the church of God: Even as I please all men in all things, not seeking mine own profit, but the profit of many, that they may be saved." (Acts 10v32&33).

To those *who are saved*, what a wonderful liberty we have in Christ! "Therefore I say unto you, Take no thought for your life, what ye shall eat, or what ye shall drink; nor yet for your body, what ye shall put on. Is not the life more than meat, and the body than raiment? Behold the fowls of the air: for they sow not, neither do they reap, nor gather into barns; yet your heavenly Father feedeth them. Are ye not much better than they?" (Matt. 6v25&26). How reassuring are the words of verse 34: "Take therefore no thought for the morrow: for the morrow shall take thought for the things of itself. Sufficient unto the day is the evil thereof."

When His children pray: "Give us this day our daily bread," (Matt. 6v11), they can be sure of a positive answer to that request. In Genesis, when famine swept Egypt and surrounding lands, the Lord provided for His people through Joseph who had been sold into slavery, but miraculously rose to become Pharaoh's deputy! Later, in the Book of Exodus, when the Children of Israel fled from Egypt, the Lord provided daily bread in the form of that mysterious food 'manna,' which we are told "they did eat... for forty years, until they came to a land inhabited;" (Ex. 16v35). After some time, we are told that the people became tired of it... "We remember the fish, which we did eat in Egypt freely; the cucumbers, and the melons, and the leeks, and the onions, and the garlick: But now our soul is dried away: there is nothing at all, beside this manna, before our eyes." (Num. 11v5&6). Despite these complaints about the manna, I have no doubt that it was filled with every vitamin known to man - and more besides, since its source was divine. In fact, in Psalm 78v25 it is referred to as 'angel's food.' We learn how quails were sent, and ultimately, how judgement fell, upon those who 'lusted.' (Num. 11v33&34).

More proof that the Lord will attend to this basic need for food, for His children, is contained in Psalm 37v25... "I have been young, and now am old; yet have I not seen the righteous forsaken, nor his seed begging bread." Also... "The young lions do lack, and suffer hunger: but they that seek the Lord shall not want any good thing." (Psalm 34v10). Sometimes, though, in our world there are nations where multitudes of people die from malnutrition. Perhaps the nation's leaders may be truly evil and engaged in wrongful conflict. Regardless of this, Christians are exhorted to help the starving of such nations, even if those nations are our enemies... "Therefore if thine enemy hunger, feed him; if he thirst, give him drink: for in so doing thou shalt heap coals of fire on his head. Be not overcome of evil, but overcome evil with good." (Rom. 12v20&21). Also, such nations may be inhabited by our brothers and sisters in the Lord, in addition to babies and innocent children. James tells us: "If a brother or sister be naked, and destitute of daily food, And one of you say unto them, Depart in peace, be ye warmed and filled; notwithstanding ye give them not those things which are needful to the body; what doth it profit? Even so faith, if it hath not works, is dead, being alone." (James 2v15-17). In Isaiah 58v10&11 we read of the fruits of His children who help the hungry, both spiritually and physically: "And if thou draw out thy soul to the hungry, and satisfy the afflicted soul; then shall thy light rise in obscurity, and thy darkness be as the noonday: And the Lord shall guide thee continually, and satisfy thy soul in drought, and make fat thy bones: and thou shalt be like a watered garden, and like a spring of water, whose waters fail not. And they that shall be of thee shall build the old waste places: thou shalt raise up the foundations of many generations; and thou shalt be called, The repairer of the breach, The restorer of paths to dwell in."

It is in Isaiah Chapter 58 that we also read of 'fasting.' For the Christian this must be something which is accompanied by much prayer - potentially a very effective tool against the devil. As has been said, the unregenerate cannot make themselves worthy before God by fasting, but Christians may certainly feel led of the Lord to 'fast and pray,' so that His will be accomplished. In Matthew chapter 17 we read of a distraught father who came to beseech Jesus for his son, who was possessed by the devil and who often fell into the fire or water. The disciples, unable to cast the devil out, asked Jesus why this was so. Jesus proceeded to tell them that it was because of their unbelief and lack of faith (Verse 20). He added... "Howbeit this kind goeth not out but by *prayer and fasting.*" (Verse 21). In Matthew chapter 6 (part of the well known 'Sermon on the Mount'), Jesus gives us instructions for fasting... "Moreover when ye fast, be not, as the hypocrites, of a sad countenance: for they disfigure their faces, that they may appear unto men to fast. Verily I say unto you, They have their reward. But thou, when thou fastest, anoint thine head, and wash thy face; That thou appear not unto men to fast, but unto thy Father which is in secret: and thy Father, which seeth in secret, shall reward thee openly." (Verses 16-18).

Undoubtedly fasting with prayer is commendable in the life of a Christian who seeks God's will, but outside of Christ physical and psychological problems abound in today's western world, where food is concerned. While obesity is a problem in developed nations, others die from malnutrition in third world societies - and surely only Jesus can perfectly heal the victims of bulimia and anorexia? He will also protect those who trust in Him from that other problem - the evils in our food industry! Those who have made the Lord "their refuge and fortress" are encouraged by David in his lovely Psalm 91, from which I quote verses 9-16... "Because thou hast made the Lord, which is my refuge, even the most High, thy habitation; There shall no evil befall thee, neither shall any plague come nigh thy dwelling. For he shall give his angels charge over thee, to keep thee in all thy ways. They shall bear thee up in their hands, lest thou dash thy foot against a stone. Thou shalt tread upon the lion and the adder: the young lion and the dragon shalt thou trample under feet. Because he hath set his love upon me, therefore will I deliver him: I will set him on high, because he hath known my name. He shall call upon me, and I will answer him: I will be with him in trouble; I will deliver him, and honour him. With long life will I satisfy him, and shew him my salvation."

Later that evening, after the rush of the day, and having cooked a (basic but wholesome) dinner for the family, I settled down to read the 'list of affected food.' Scanning the newspaper carefully, I sighed with relief, realising that I had never bought any of those particular products! Even if I had, I still felt that reassurance from the Lord that He would protect us. Resolving to use the discernment He had given me, with regard to food, or any other issue, I fell peacefully asleep that night in the knowledge that... "Behold, he that keepeth Israel shall neither slumber nor sleep. The Lord is thy keeper: the Lord is thy shade upon thy right hand. The sun shall not smite thee by day, nor the moon by night. The Lord shall preserve thee from all evil: he shall preserve thy soul. The Lord shall preserve thy going out and thy coming in from this time forth, and even for evermore." (Ps. 121v4-8).

In days of yore the manna fell,
Or in the desert sprang a well,
"Fear not my servants," saith thy Guide,
"My love and mercy will provide."

Strawberries – now available in more than one Irish season!

(5)

"It's an Ill Wind that Blows Nobody Good"
(John 3v7&8)

March 1st- March15th

As dusk fell, storm clouds had already gathered and a gale warning had been issued. Later that night the mighty wind grew more fierce, so that the electricity power supply and telephone links were cut to our area. Before pulling down the bedroom blinds, I looked out with concern as a large flowerpot flew rapidly past the window - somehow an ominous sign of the night that lay ahead. The trees, still stark after the harsh winter, bent over in the wake of the fierce gusts. I was glad that I had brought in the washing from the line, for in the morning I may have found them in our neighbours' garden - a quarter of a mile away! Extreme weather conditions are rare in Ireland, but in recent years storms have grown more common in winter and early spring, wreaking havoc, especially in coastal areas. Having blown out the last flickering candle, we retired for the night.

Often throughout that night I was to be awakened by loud rumbles of thunder, and lightening flashing across the bedroom walls. The wind rushed wildly through the trees, and heavy rain pelted relentlessly against our windows and roof. I had no doubt that the sea, just a few miles away, would be foaming angrily at the rocks and cliffs, its waves mounting high and crashing in on the shore. In the darkness of the night, I prayed for those far out at sea ... "The voice of thy thunder was in the heaven: the lightnings lightened the world: the earth trembled and shook. Thy way is in the sea, and thy path in the great waters, and thy footsteps are not known. Thou leddest thy people like a flock by the hand of Moses and Aaron." (Psalm 77v18-20).

With daybreak came calm but also chaotic evidence of the night's storm. March had certainly 'come in like a lion!' As I drove the children to school, we encountered great branches and then an entire tree forced me to the other side of the road. Rivers were bursting their banks and the small village close to our home was

31

beginning to look like a Venetian scene in winter. Some flooded cars had been abandoned, and as I tried various routes to reach the school, I knew that my efforts were in vain, for the nearby estuary had burst its banks. Returning home, we were glad of the warmth of the old oil-fired Aga and the friendly whistle of the kettle, as electricity had not yet been restored. From the radio I learned of the previous night's devastation and marvelled at how wind, an invisible force of unknown origin, could produce such visible effects. Then I thought on that familiar verse in John 3v8: "The wind bloweth where it listeth, and thou hearest the sound thereof, but canst not tell whence it cometh, and whither it goeth: so is every one that is born of the Spirit."

The wind in this lovely portion of scripture reminds me of a gentle breeze, as opposed to a fierce storm. When I was a baby, my mother used to position my pram under a large tree in summer, as the breeze blowing gently through the leaves fascinated me. Eventually I would fall asleep - giving her a well-deserved break! I have always loved the sound of the wind but sometimes I have been afraid, when tossed to and fro on an angry sea or while sitting petrified on a long flight while turbulence persists.

The Person of the Holy Spirit has been compared throughout scripture to the wind, in all its facets. In Acts 2v2-4 we read: "And suddenly there came a sound from heaven as of a rushing mighty wind, and it filled all the house where they were sitting. And there appeared unto them cloven tongues like as of fire, and it set upon each of them. And they were all filled with the Holy Ghost, and began to speak with other tongues, as the Spirit gave them utterance." How wonderful that those of every nation under heaven (Acts 2v5) who were gathered in Jerusalem at that time could now hear the gospel in their own language! At the tower of Babel (Gen. 11v9) arrogant men were thrown into confusion, for they could no longer understand each other's language - but now humble souls were given the instant ability to speak other languages, so that the joyful news of salvation could be spread throughout the nations! And so the Holy Spirit, like a mighty rushing wind had wrought amazing changes in its wake, turning the hearts of the people to fear the living God and putting a desire in their hearts to be filled with His spirit and to be ready for His coming again.

When faced with seemingly dangerous conditions on an aircraft, people will inevitably attempt to reach out to God in their own way. Once on a flight from Athens, I was amused to watch a Greek Cypriot lady nervously finger beads while whispering prayers. As a young person without Christ, I had not yet learned the essential truth that "the fear of the Lord is the beginning of wisdom." (Prov.9v10). But the Greek Cypriot lady had not yet learned the truth contained in those inspired words of Paul in Acts 17v22-29. People are (naturally) greatly troubled by what even the most agnostic sceptics amongst insurance brokers refer to as "acts of God." Indeed, very often the Lord uses such acts to draw souls to Himself.

When Christians pray fervently for the salvation of souls, the Holy Spirit moves upon the lives of those individuals as a convicting, turbulent force. (James 5v16). Consequently, events will unleash on those lives, as the Lord seeks (by various appropriate means) to win these souls for whom He died. Therefore, "the wind bloweth where it listeth," but if there is to be new life, then each person must be responsive to the workings of the Holy Spirit upon his or her life.

In Revelation 7v1 we read: "And after these things I saw four angels standing on the four corners of the earth, holding the four winds of the earth, that the wind should not blow on the earth, nor on the sea, nor on any tree." An atmosphere where there is not even a tiny breeze seems incredible! However some day, in the same way that God will instruct those four angels to 'hold' the north, south, east and west winds, He will also withdraw His Holy Spirit from His convicting work on the hearts of individuals. "My Spirit shall not always strive with man," we learn in Genesis 6v3. (I wish to say that while I was typing these very words just now - the electricity went off and I was left, very suddenly, with a blank screen! This, I believe, happened for a reason, and illustrates perfectly the words of Genesis 6v3. I also wish to thank God that He restored electricity after lunch, so that a morning's work had not been lost. Now I was able to continue where I had left off, despite having not saved the extract on my old computer!)

Today we still live in 'the day of His grace.' Are you fortunate enough to be still listening to His convicting voice? Some day that still small voice of conviction will cease. That day for anyone still outside of Christ could even be today, and so we read … "Seek ye the Lord while He may be found, call ye upon Him while He is near." (Isaiah 55v6). Also, Christians are commanded to "grieve not the Holy Spirit" in Ephesians 4v30. We are gravely warned to be ready for His coming - which may be at any time. (Mark 13v35-37).

That stormy night, and many others, are outstanding reminders of God's omnipotence in the universe. A short time later I heard of one terrified soul who acknowledged that this must have been the work of the living God, 'who is angry with us.' Was it not an 'ill wind' that resulted in Jonah being swallowed by a whale, but with the restoration of calm his shipmates made vows to the Lord? (Jonah 1v15&16). "For, lo, he that formeth the mountains, and createth the wind, and declareth unto man what is his thought, that maketh the morning darkness, and treadeth upon the high places of the earth, The Lord, The God of hosts, is his name." (Amos 4v13).

Let us call upon this loving Creator, Saviour and Comforter, whom Elijah found - not in the great strong wind, or the earthquake or fire, but in a "still small voice." (1Kings 19v11-13). The voice that commanded: "Let there be light," (Gen 1v3); the voice that encouraged the prophets of old; and called Samuel three times (1Sam.3v8); the voice that rebuked the wind, saying "peace be still," (Mark 4v39); the voice of love that said: "It is finished." (John 19v30) - This still small voice calls yet above the thundering storms of life for you and me today. "Be of good cheer; it is I; be not afraid…." He cried to His disciples and "Come," he said to Peter, as he took those first positive steps of faith upon the water. (Matt. 14v27-29)

That wonderful day when "there came a sound from heaven, as of a rushing mighty wind," (Acts 2v2) is described by the prophet Joel some eight hundred years earlier: "And it shall come to pass in the last days, saith God, I will pour out of my Spirit upon all flesh: and your sons and your daughters shall prophesy, and your young men shall see visions, and your old men shall dream dreams…" (Joel 2v28; Acts 2v17). As that day (approximately AD. 33) is described as being "in the last days," surely we, in these days, are living *very* much in "the last days?" It is my ernest and urgent prayer that those who read this, being outside of Christ, would cry: "Lord, save us: we perish." (Matt. 8v25). Surely, the "Prince of

Peace," (Isaiah 9v6), who "rebuked the winds and the sea," (Matt. 8v26), can touch your life with a peace and calm, such as you have never known before? The seas of life may still foam angrily around us, but Jesus is our "anchor," our hope "until the day break, and the shadows flee away..." (Solomon's Song 2v17). "Which hope we have as an anchor of the soul, both sure and stedfast, and which entereth into that within the veil; Whither the forerunner is for us entered, even Jesus, made an high priest for ever after the order of Mel-chis-ed-ec." (Heb. 6v19&20). "Therefore being justified by faith, we have peace with God through our Lord Jesus Christ." (Romans 5v1)

There is a wind that no one knows
From whence it comes or where it blows,
But when it touches souls of men,
The Spirit whispers… "Born Again."
(John 3v8)

The River Nanny flooding lands near Julianstown, Co. Meath.

35

(6)

"And These Three Are One..."
(1John 5v7&8)

(March 16th- March 31st)

The late afternoon was cold as we clambered over the rusty gate which led from our field into the back lane. Walking swiftly in order to keep warm, we soon found ourselves in the environs of an old deserted farmhouse and its out-dwellings. We had become familiar with the latter since moving here some years previously and this walk down the narrow lane with its high hedges, through the old farm - and onwards to green fields, a forest and glen, was one that we enjoyed in all seasons.

Now it was early spring and the sharp east wind blew fiercely through the derelict barns. "This place looks worse every time I see it," my young daughter commented.

"Yes," I agreed, "look at the roof on that shed. It seems to be on the verge of collapsing!" The two-storey farmhouse itself didn't appear to be in as bad condition, but even *it* looked the worse for wear. In recent years its dilapidated windows and doors had been hammered over with tin sheeting. As we stood in the overgrown walled garden for a moment my thoughts, as always, dwelt on the folks who once lived there. Who were they, and why did this house with its garden and farm buildings now lie sadly abandoned? Dying snowdrops were still in evidence and some primroses had begun to emerge with the first rays of spring sunshine. The old ivy-covered walls that had once been witness to the laughter and tears of daily life now had a decidedly melancholy look about them. Briars had started to grow in a tangle through holes in the slates, and starlings had nested in the cracked chimney pots. The wind whistled and murmured in the evergreens and a shed door swung mournfully to and fro on its hinges. Walking away from the house, we made our way onwards through the deserted farmyard. In one shed we observed, again, the ancient butter churn and in another, the remains of a rusty plough which would once have been drawn by sturdy horses. A cobweb-covered saddle hung on a cold stone wall, and every now and then it would be disturbed by the wind, humming incessantly though the derelict outhouse.

Leaving the melancholy farm behind us, we headed on to a lush meadow and our familiar little stream and pond where, annually, we would discover the frogs' spawns of early spring. The glen, beautiful in any season, lay invitingly ahead. But today the distant sea looked cold and grey, as it blended with the horizon. Making our way downhill past some grazing cattle, we came at last to our 'special place.' There, resplendent amongst the great trees, was our little waterfall, full and cascading after the winter rains. Cupping my hands, I drank a little and then sat on the branch of a great oak, absorbing the sounds, sights and smells of the birth of another spring.

"That water will run dry, come summer, Mum," shouted my daughter, above the noise of rushing water. "Oh look here - some shamrock!" Reaching for one delicate little trefoil, I observed it in detail. 'Yes,' I thought, 'three heart-shaped tiny leaves, equal in size and beauty - but one sturdy, healthy stem.' I could not help but think of those equally beautiful, very significant words... "For there are three that bear record in heaven, the Father, the Word, and the Holy Ghost: and these three are one. And there are three that bear witness in earth, the spirit, the water, and the blood: and these three agree in one." (1John 5v7&8).

Gathering a cluster of pretty green shamrocks, I climbed the bank once more and cast a backward glance at the rushing waterfall, glinting in a pale ray of evening sunshine. Looking at it longingly, I already felt thirsty again! "Whosoever drinketh of this water shall thirst again," said Jesus to the woman at the well, "But whosoever drinketh of the water that I shall give him shall never thirst; but the water that I shall give him shall be in him a well of water springing up into everlasting life." (St. John 4v13&14). How marvellous that the spiritually satisfying 'water of life' is available to all who will come! "Behold, God is my salvation; I will trust, and not be afraid: for the Lord Jehova is my strength and my song; he also is become my salvation. Therefore with joy shall ye draw water out of the wells of salvation." (Isaiah 12v2&3). "I am Alpha and Omega, the beginning and the end. I will give unto him that is athirst of the fountain of the water of life freely." (Rev.21v6).

'Alpha and Omega,' I thought, as we strolled home, 'surely only God is Alpha and Omega, the beginning and the ending?' Yet Jesus, in Rev. 1v17&18 tells John… "Fear not; *I am the first and the last: I am he that liveth, and was dead; and, behold, I am alive for evermore, Amen; and have the keys of hell and of death.*" Throughout the centuries until this present day, there have been those who deny the deity of the Lord Jesus Christ. My thoughts travelled back to another spring day, when I opened the door to a well-dressed gentleman with a large briefcase. Showing me some beautiful pictures, he politely explained to me that I could be a citizen of 'a bright New World, where terrible events like wars and accidents didn't happen any more.' I, in turn, explained to him that I had put my faith in One, Jesus Christ, who had died for me - but who was alive forevermore. As a result of this my inheritance was a mansion in heaven, and "eye hath not seen, nor ear heard, neither have entered into the heart of man, the things which God hath prepared for them that love him." (1Cor. 2v9). There followed a debate on the deity of Christ. Glancing at 1John 5v7&8, he said: "yes, I see that - but didn't you know that your version of the Bible is spurious? We worship God. There is but one God." Now some years later, I looked again at my little cluster of green shamrocks and smiled. Yes, one God, but three Persons!

The man that I had spoken to that day was of the opinion that Jesus was 'Michael the Archangel.' "So you don't think that Jesus should be worshipped?" I asked.

"No" he replied. "Only God should be worshipped." Later I read: "God, who at sundry times and divers manners spake in time past unto the fathers by the prophets, Hath in these last days spoken unto us by his Son, whom he hath appointed heir of all things, *by whom also he made the worlds;* Who being the brightness of his glory, and the express image of his person, and upholding all things by the word of his power, when he had by himself purged our sins, sat down on the right hand of the Majesty on high; Being made *so much better that the angels, as he hath by inheritance obtained a more excellent name that they.* For unto which of the angels said he at any time, Thou art my Son, this day have I begotten thee? And again, I will be to him a Father, and he shall be to me a Son? And again, when he bringeth in the first begotten into the world, he saith, *And let all the angels of God worship him.* And of the angels he saith, Who maketh his angels spirits, and his ministers a flame of fire. *But unto the Son he saith, Thy throne, O God, is for ever and ever: a sceptre of righteousness is the sceptre of thy kingdom."* (Heb. 1v1-8). This entire chapter is devoted to upholding the deity of our Lord Jesus Christ. If only those who deny this could see it!

In Genesis 1v26 we read: "And God said, Let *us* make man in *our* image, after *our* likeness..." Later in Genesis 3v22 God says... "Behold the man is become as one of *us,* to know good and evil...", and in Genesis 11v7 the little word 'us' is again introduced... "Go to, let *us go* down..." How wonderful that our Creator is also our Redeemer! "He was in the world, and the world was made by him, and the world knew him not." (John 1v10). "And now, O Father, glorify thou me with thine own self with the glory which I had with thee before the world was." (John 17v5). "In the beginning was the Word, and the Word was with God, and the Word *was* God. The same was in the beginning *with* God. All things were made by him; and without him was not anything made that was made." (John 1v1-3). Further proof that the "Word" is Jesus, is contained in John 1v14... "And the Word was made flesh, and dwelt among us, (and we beheld his glory, the glory as of the only begotten of the Father,) full of grace and truth."

What a privilege (but also a great challenge) it must have been to have known Jesus in person, as He walked upon this earth performing numerous miracles! The hands of the Creator and the hands of the Great Healer who touched Peter's mother-in-law (Matthew 8v15), and many others, are those same hands that were pierced for our transgressions! Acts 20v28 gives us further evidence of His deity. Here, Paul instructs the elders of Ephesus... "Take heed therefore unto yourselves, and to all the flock, over the which the Holy Ghost hath made you overseers, to feed the church of *God, which he hath purchased with his own blood."* It is interesting to note that this verse, does, in fact, refer to all three persons of the Trinity! Jesus, in that beautiful Chapter 14 of St. John's Gospel, refers very much to His Father - and also to "the Comforter" (verse 16), or the "Spirit of truth," (verse 17).

That the Holy Spirit is a person, is unquestionable, since Jesus refers to him as "He." In the following verse all three persons of the

Trinity are again wonderfully portrayed... "But the Comforter, which is the Holy Ghost, whom the Father will send in my name, he shall teach you all things, and bring all things to your remembrance, whatsoever I have said unto you." (St. John 14v26).

Homeward bound, once more we reached the old deserted farm. Yes, the law of 'Universal Decay' was very much in evidence there! I was always fascinated by the fact that any building left to itself will slowly, but surely, start to disintegrate. I have seen many examples of these unoccupied dwellings, especially in rural areas. Even the ruins of what were once the grand mansions of aristocracy often lie miserably derelict and sadly dangerous in their decadence. Surely without the indwelling presence of the Holy Spirit, we too would face ultimate destruction? Unless the Lord returns in our lifetime, these earthly bodies of ours will some day die and decay... "but if the Spirit of him that raised up Jesus from the dead dwell in you, he that raised up Christ from the dead shall also quicken your mortal bodies by his Spirit that dwelleth in you." (Rom. 8v11). However, if we are destitute of His quickening presence - death and eternal destruction await us. In Romans 8v12&13, Christians are warned... "Therefore, brethren, we are debtors, not to the flesh, to live after the flesh. For if ye live after the flesh, ye shall die: but if ye through the Spirit do mortify the deeds of the body, ye shall live."

A man, rich in prestige and the things of this world, but without Christ, is as without hope and decadent, as the ruins of any great house. But if he can humbly come to the Lord, and truly say with the Psalmist... "Purge me with hyssop, and I shall be clean: wash me, and I shall be whiter than snow," (Psalm 51v7), then the Lord will come in strength, and fill that heart with His presence. "And I say unto you, Ask, and it shall be given you; seek, and ye shall find; knock, and it shall be opened unto you." (Luke 11v9).

In Psalm 51, David the backslider acknowledges his transgressions, and pleads for mercy... "Hide thy face from my sins, and blot out all mine iniquities. Create in me a clean heart, O God; and renew a right spirit within me. Cast me not away from thy presence; and take not thy holy spirit from me." (Verses 9-11).

To a restored David, his joy and confidence was in the Lord - in all His fullness. What if David had not repented of his sin in the matter of Uriah the Hittite? (2Samuel 11) Ezekiel 3v20 informs us that... "When a righteous man doth turn from his righteousness, and commit iniquity, and I lay a stumblingblock before him, he shall die: because thou hast not given him warning, he shall die in his sin, and his righteousness which he hath done shall not be remembered; but his blood will I require at thine hand." Here we may see clearly that the Lord's servant, if he does not repent, will most certainly die in his sin. Thank God for Nathan, the prophet, who warned David in a parable (2Samuel 12). In Verse 13 of this chapter, David acknowledges his sin, with a repentant heart. Surely Nathan could identify with the following verse in Ezekiel 3v21..."Nevertheless if thou warn the righteous man, that the righteous sin not, and he doth not sin, he shall surely live, because he is warned; also thou hast delivered thy soul." How marvellous that a restored David went on to write the Psalms which continue to be a source of inspiration and comfort to mankind through the ages! Throughout these we may see many references to Father, Son and Holy Spirit.

Psalm 51 refers to Nathan's visit of admonition to David, and it is also a Psalm which deals very much with the Holy Spirit. Psalm 104, on the other hand, is one which declares the glory of the Creator... "The high hills are a refuge for the wild goats; and the rocks for the conies. He appointed the moon for seasons: the sun knoweth his going down. Thou maketh darkness, and it is night: wherein all the beasts of the forest do creep forth." (Verses 18-20). "The glory of the Lord shall endure for ever: the Lord shall rejoice in his works." (Verse31). Psalm 72, in its entirety, refers to the promised Messiah... "His name shall endure forever: his name shall be continued as long as the sun: and men shall be blessed in him: all nations shall call him blessed." (Verse 17). Psalm 2v7 mentions "The Son"... "I will declare the decree: the Lord hath said unto me, Thou art my Son; this day have I begotten thee." Finally in verse 12 of this Psalm we read: "Kiss the Son, lest he be angry, and ye perish from the way, when his wrath is kindled but a little. Blessed are all they that put their trust in him." Psalm 22 is prophetic of the Lord's crucifixion. The poignant cry in Verse 1 echoes down the centuries from Mark 15v34... "My God, my God, why hast thou forsaken me?"

"God, forsaken of God," said Martin Luther - "almost inconceivable to the human mind!" Yet, as believers, we accept this wonder, by faith - and in the knowledge that this was prophesied long ago by David, Isaiah and many others. Of His birth Isaiah prophesies… "Therefore the Lord himself shall give you a sign; Behold, a virgin shall conceive, and bear a son, and shall call his name Immanuel." (Isaiah 7v14). Psalm 22v16-18 prophesies His death… "For dogs have compassed me: the assembly of the wicked have inclosed me: they pieced my hands and my feet. I may tell all my bones: they look and stare upon me. They part my garments among them, and cast lots upon my vesture." His glorious resurrection is indicated in Psalm 16v10… "For thou wilt not leave my soul in hell; neither wilt thou suffer thine Holy One to see corruption." All this He suffered for us, for our redemption… "To redeem them that were under the law, that we might receive the adoption of sons. And because ye are sons, God hath sent forth the Spirit of his Son into your hearts, crying, Abba, Father. Wherefore thou art no more a servant, but a son; and if a son, then an heir of God through Christ." (Gal. 4v5-7). Oh, that these earthly bodies of ours would be filled with the presence of His Holy Spirit!

"Some day, Mum," said my daughter, as we walked past the derelict house in the twilight, "I would love to buy the old house and restore it. If I got in there, I know that I could make it really beautiful." I smiled, thinking…

"Yes," I whispered. "Then it would no longer be under the 'law of universal decay.' It would be occupied by someone who truly cared for it. No longer would the wind whine through broken slates and the old staircase creak with decay, awaiting the day when it would be destroyed forever! Once more those walls would be witness to love and fullness of life."

So it is, when we come to the Father, in the precious name of His Son Jesus Christ, and are indwelt by the fullness of His Spirit. Turning to my daughter, I replied… "You know, if I had the money I would buy that house for you." Jesus said: "If ye then, being evil, know how to give good gifts unto your children: how much more shall your heavenly Father give the Holy Spirit to them that ask him?" (Luke11v13). "And whatsoever ye shall ask in my name, that will I do, that the Father may be glorified in the Son. If ye shall ask any thing in my name, I will do it. If ye love me, keep my commandments. And I will pray the Father, and he shall give you another Comforter, that he may abide with you for ever; Even the Spirit of truth; whom the world cannot receive, because it seeth him not, neither knoweth him: but ye know him; for he dwelleth with you, and shall be in you." (John 14v13-17). Each one of us, as individuals, can claim these great promises and apply them to our own hearts, if we but surrender all to God – the Three in One. Praise His name! Why not seek His loving face and ask Him to meet you at the point of *your* need today?

One stem, one root, one source,
One single mighty force,
And from this One, the Heavenly Host:
Father, Son, and Holy Ghost.
Creator, Saviour, Spirit of Love,
Almighty mercy from above:
The voice that cried: "Let there be light."
Cried "It is finished" in the night.
O Spirit who raised my Lord from death -
Breathe on those who read, thy breath,
That they might find that narrow way
That leads to perfect, endless, Day.

A Visitor from Poland
(1John 2v2)

(April 1st- April 15th)

I was almost certain that I heard the doorbell ringing over the noise of clattering pots and pans, as I prepared for dinner. "Who could that be, at this time?" I sighed as I set everything aside and dried my hands. "We don't often get visitors out here in the 'sticks!'"

"There's somebody at the door, Mum," shouted my youngest daughter. "It's this man with a big bag... don't know who he is."

"Could *you* not answer it?" I replied. "You know I'm busy!"

"Oh no Mum - you'd better."

"Ok," I said resignedly.

Hurrying to the door, I opened it to find a young man standing there. Somehow, he looked foreign, like one of the many East Europeans who have come to live in Ireland in recent years. In his hand there was indeed 'a big bag.' "Allo," he greeted me with a friendly grin. "I am from Kraków in Poland. My mother, she is very ill. She needs operation. I am art student from University in Kraków, and now," he added, opening the bag, "I want to sell my art, to pay for her operation." One by one, he produced sketches from the big bag. "Very nice!" I said, temporarily forgetting about the dinner. He showed me impressive scenes of his native land: traditional houses, churches, landscapes... and then two pretty kittens in a basket. "I like this one," I said, with a smile. (I've always had a 'soft spot' for the feline species!) "How much?" I inquired. After a little good-humoured bargaining we agreed on a reasonable sum. Averting my eyes, he pocketed it, thanked me and made his way out onto the roadway. "I hope your mother will be alright!" I shouted after him. "Now, back to cooking the dinner," I sighed.

"Dinner... I should have offered that poor young man some dinner," I groaned. There had been no sign of a car, and he had probably walked a long way. I felt so mean about bargaining with him, especially with his mother so ill in Kraków. Why didn't I give him the full amount that he had asked for? Just then my older daughters, who had been out for a walk, returned. "Yes, we met him coming up the road. We didn't like the look of him at all," they said, when I showed them the picture - which they didn't take much notice of! It was at dinner that my youngest daughter noticed it. "That's not a sketch, Mum!" she exclaimed. "That's not even a print - it's a photocopy made to look like a sketch!"

"You've been done again!" my husband piped up.

Annoyed, I muttered… "Oh well I did feel sorry for him, what with his mother in hospital, back in Kraków…"

"Oh come on, you didn't believe that, did you?" My eldest daughter giggled. "That old story's been doing the rounds for a while!"

"Well, at least I don't feel like I've cheated him, anyway." I consoled myself. Admittedly, it was very cheap for a sketch. No, it wasn't the first time that I'd been 'done' at the doorstep!

I remember another occasion, approaching Christmas, when an elderly man called to collect money on behalf of the 'Deaf Society.' I contributed something, but discovered later from a newspaper article, that the Deaf Society does not *do* door-to-door collections, and that the Gardai were investigating my caller! 'Petty' crime and deception, of one sort or another, now abounds in our society, as do the more serious crimes, such as murder. Doubtless, the amounts that I had been tricked out of were relatively small. However, the young 'artist' was being dishonest in giving me the impression that this was his work. He even showed me the palms of his hands, which he led me to believe were covered in charcoal. How naïve I was!

Sin comes in many guises and God frowns on it all, whether man differentiates between 'venial sins' or 'mortal sins' - or 'black lies' and 'white lies.' Such terms are used nowhere in God's Word, but in James 2v10&11 we read: "For whosoever shall keep the whole law, and yet offend in one point, he is guilty of all. For he that said, Do not commit adultery, said also, Do not kill. Now if thou commit no adultery, yet if thou kill, thou art become a transgressor of the law." In Leviticus 4v2, we learn that a soul can "sin through ignorance," but even this required atonement. Throughout those early books of the Old Testament, we see that a variety of innocent creatures were

45

sacrificed in order to appease God's wrath on those who had committed many types of sin and trespasses. Young bullocks, lambs, goats, pigeons and even turtle doves were offered, depending on the sin or trespass involved. But thank God, and praise His name, for that ultimate and *final* sacrifice! John the Baptist, when he saw Jesus coming said... "Behold the Lamb of God, which taketh away the sin of the world." (John 1v29).

Throughout the world, men and women and boys and girls, sadly still struggle to try and justify themselves before whoever, or whatever, they conceive to be 'God.' Unlike the animal kingdom, each member of the human race has been born with 'a conscience.' What is considered normal practice in one society may be looked on as deep sin in another, but overall God has given to each one of us 'the knowledge of good and evil.' In Titus 2v11, we learn ... "For the grace of God that bringeth salvation hath appeared to all men." Something else which each person has been born with is "original sin." In Romans 5v12, we read of that sin which we inherited from Adam... "Wherefore, as by one man sin entered into the world, and death by sin; and so death passed upon all men, *for that all have sinned.*"

A short time after my encounter with the young Polish man, I heard of the death of someone else of Polish origin, and a native of the city of Kraków: Pope John Paul II, the previous leader of the Roman Catholic Church. Somehow I linked these two individuals in my thoughts. What did these two people have in common? Not very much, some would say, apart from the fact that they were both male and originally from Kraków. However, both were also mortals who were destined to die and face judgement some day. "And as it is appointed unto men once to die, but after this the judgement: So Christ was once offered to bear the sins of many; and unto them that look for him shall he appear the second time without sin unto salvation." (Hebrews 9v27&28). Also, both had sinned at one time or another... "For all have sinned, and come short of the glory of God;" (Romans 3v23). For this reason, therefore, both needed forgiveness, and the only Person and Mediator in whom we can find redemption and forgiveness of sins, is the Person of the Lord Jesus Christ. "Neither is there salvation in any other: for there is none other name under heaven given among men, whereby we must be saved." (Acts 4v12). Very importantly, too, was the fact that Jesus loved *both* of them so much that He left the wonders and glory of Heaven, to be that all-sufficient and *final* sacrifice for them. "For this is good and acceptable in the sight of God our Saviour; Who will have *all* men to be saved, and to come unto the knowledge of the truth. For there is one God, and one Mediator between God and men, the man Christ Jesus; Who gave himself a ransom for *all*, to be testified in due time." (1Tim. 2v3-6). "For it is not possible that the blood of bulls and of goats should take away sins." (Hebrews 10v4) "Neither by the blood of goats and calves, but by his own blood he entered in *once* into the holy place, having obtained eternal redemption for us." (Hebrews 9v12)

Despite what many would have us believe, *only Jesus* was capable of being that Perfect Mediator between God and man. This was because of His very deity itself. Only *He* was immaculately conceived, and only *He* never needed forgiveness for sins - because only *He* had never sinned. "But this man, because he continueth ever, hath an unchangeable priesthood. Wherefore he is able also to save them to the uttermost that come unto God by him, seeing he ever liveth to make intercession for them. For such an high priest became us, who is holy, harmless, undefiled, separate from sinners, and made higher than the heavens;" (Hebrews 7v24-26). In 2Cor. 5v21, Paul tells us… "For He hath made him to be sin for us, who knew no sin; that we might be made the righteousness of God in him."

What a sacrifice! There has never been any like it before, and nor will there ever be again, in this world. It is no wonder that we are warned… "How shall we escape, if we neglect so great salvation…" (Hebrews 2v3). Taking a walk, between the April showers, I love to watch those new-born lambs skipping around the fields in delight, or feeding hungrily from their mothers. How harmless and innocent they are, and yet it is only the blood of Jesus, the precious Lamb of God, which can take away sin. "Forasmuch as ye know that ye were not redeemed with corruptible things, as silver and gold, from your vain conversation received by tradition from your fathers; But with the precious blood of Christ, as of a lamb without blemish and without spot:" (1Pet.1v18&19).

Every sin ever known to mankind was borne by the Lord Jesus Christ, when He suffered for us at Calvary. Whether it was the lies and deception of a young man some 2000 years later; or the dishonesty of many of our politicians; or some terrible murder - He bore our sins. "Who his own self bare our sins in his own body on the tree, that we, being dead to sins, should live unto righteousness: by whose stripes ye were healed." (1Pet.2v24). Smitten and crucified by man, forsaken by God the Father, He descended into the very depths of hell - but on the third day He arose again! "For Christ also hath *once* suffered for sins, the just for the unjust, that he might bring us to God, being put to death in the flesh, but quickened by the Spirit: By which also he went and preached unto the spirits in prison:" (1Pet.3v18&19). "Blessed be the God and Father of our Lord Jesus Christ, which according to his abundant mercy hath begotten us again unto a lively hope by the resurrection of Jesus Christ from the dead." (1Pet. 1v3)

It is in His triumphant resurrection that we have the victory! Why then, do we "seek the living amongst the dead?" When Jesus uttered those three significant words…"It is finished," (John 19v30), He meant it, in every sense of those words. "By the which will we are sanctified through the offering of the body of Jesus Christ *once for all.* And every priest standeth daily ministering and offering oftentimes the same sacrifices, which can never take away sins: But this man, after he had offered *one sacrifice for sins for ever, sat down on the right hand of God*; From henceforth expecting till his enemies be made his footstool. For *by one offering* he hath perfected for ever them that are sanctified." (Hebrews 10v10-14). What a defining moment in the history of mankind! Finished, the necessity for animal sacrifices - finished the striving and the rituals! For those who repent, turn from sin and put their trust in the Blessed Risen Saviour, He says… "I will put my laws into their hearts, and in their minds will I write them; And their sins and iniquities will I remember no more. Now where remission of these is, there is no more offering for sin." (Hebrews 10v16-18). When I study that wonderful book of Hebrews, which declares the perfect sufficiency of Christ's death and resurrection for us, I am amazed at the number of times that the little words 'one' and 'once' are used, particularly in Hebrews 9&10! Surely the Word of God speaks for itself?

A short time after meeting that young Polish man, I bought a nice frame for the 'sketch.' Unfortunately, this had the effect of making it look even *less* authentic. Consequently I had the following thoughts... There is nothing that we can do to 'dress,' or cover up sin. Nowhere in the Bible are we told that 'God does not see our sins.' After we have become Christians, the devil will shortly rear 'his ugly head,' and sin is something that must be dealt with by our Lord Jesus Christ. "My little children," states John in 1John 2v1-3, "these things write I unto you, that ye sin not. And *if* any man sin, we have an advocate with the Father, Jesus Christ the righteous: And he is the propitiation for our sins: and not for ours only, but also for the sins of the whole world. And hereby we do know that we know him, if we keep his commandments."

Praise God for that Advocate, who now sits at the right hand of God the Father! (Colossians 3v1). Praise God for His atoning blood... "But if we walk in the light, as he is in the light, we have fellowship one with another, and the blood of Jesus Christ his Son cleanseth us from *all* sin." (1John 1v7). There were two criminals who hung on either side of Jesus that crucifixion day, and in a sense they represent all the world of lost sinners. He loved (and died for) both of them - but one rejected Him and one trusted in Him for eternal life. And Jesus said to the one who trusted Him: "Verily I say unto thee, To day shalt thou be with me in Paradise." (Luke 23v43). He loved you, the reader, whoever you are, and He died for you too, in order that "your sins and iniquities, He would remember no more." (Heb. 10v17). Like the thief who made the right choice on that fateful day, you too can start this very day - on the road that leads to Paradise. And when we walk with Jesus, a little bit of Paradise can be ours - even amidst the sorrows and troubles of this world! "Ye that love the Lord, hate evil: he preserveth the souls of his saints; he delivereth them out of the hand of the wicked. Light is sown for the righteous, and gladness for the upright in heart. Rejoice in the Lord, ye righteous; and give thanks at the remembrance of his holiness." (Psalm 97v10-12).

Perhaps I shall never see that young Pole again, but I would dearly love to - in heaven. I regret very much not having taken the opportunity to be a witness to him. ("And others save with fear, pulling them out of the fire; hating even the garment spotted by the flesh" - Jude v23). Yet I pray that he will find the truth and that his sins (for which my Lord died) will be forgiven. If Jesus had not died for us, we would be the heirs of eternal misery. But thank God that "Christ hath redeemed us from the curse of the law, being made a curse for us; for it is written, Cursed is every one that hangeth on a tree; That the blessing of Abraham might come on the Gentiles through Jesus Christ; that we might receive the promise of the Spirit through faith." (Gal. 3v13&14).

"Behold, he cometh with clouds; and every eye shall see him, and they also which pierced him: and all kindreds of the earth shall wail because of him. Even so, Amen." (Rev. 1v7). The eyes of Bishops, and Kings, and Queens, and peasants shall see His coming in the clouds, and who shall not be ashamed at His coming? Only those who have been washed in the blood of the Lamb, and "who walk in the light, as he is in the light." (1John 1v7). To those who know Him not He says... "Believe on the Lord Jesus Christ, and thou shalt be saved, and thy house." (Acts 16v31). To the Christian He says... "And now, little children, abide in him; that, when he shall appear, we may have confidence, and not be ashamed before him at his coming. If ye know that he is righteous, ye know that every one that doeth righteousness is born of him." (1John 2v28&29). He is able to save - and to save to the uttermost! In our daily walk with Him, He can keep us from falling for there is "power in the blood." "For thou hast delivered my soul from death: wilt not thou deliver my feet from falling, that I may walk before God in the light of the living?" (Psalm 56v13). Nothing has inspired the soul of man like the death and resurrection of the Lord Jesus Christ. No other religion or system of belief in the world encompasses such beauty, such a wonder, such love, as His awesome sacrifice for the redemption of the human race. Throughout the ages it has inspired poets, hymnists, artists, philosophers, composers and musicians. But only those who have humbled themselves before Him can identify with the words of Paul in Philippians 3v7-9... "But what things were gain to me, those I counted loss for Christ. Yea doubtless, and I do count all things but loss for the excellency of the knowledge of Christ Jesus my Lord: for whom I have suffered the loss of all things, and do count them but dung, that I may win Christ, And be found in him, not having mine own righteousness, which is of the law, but that which is through the faith of Christ, the righteousness which is of God by faith:"

Oh that all, both small and great (Rev. 20v12) would "know him, and the power of his resurrection, and the fellowship of his sufferings, being made conformable unto his death..." (Phil. 3v10). "Surely he hath borne our griefs, and carried our sorrows: yet we did esteem him stricken, smitten of God, and afflicted. But he was wounded for our transgressions, he was bruised for our iniquities: the chastisement of our peace was upon him; and with his stripes we are healed." (Isaiah 53v4&5)

Perhaps some day this transient life,
With all its sorrow, joy and strife,
Like a vapour, will vanish away,
This earthly frame beneath the clay,
My name forgotten quietly,
With the death of those who loved me.
But there is One who will remember me -
Surely the King of Immortality?
He, suffering, died that we should live forever,
His blood a cleansing, flowing river,
His rising conquered sin and death forever -
For all mankind - the "whosoever,"
O Lord thy victory is mine forever!

(8)

"Performance Subject to Growing Conditions…"
A Lesson from the Garden.
(Matthew 13)

(April 16th- April 30th)

It was one of those mornings when all of nature seemed to sing the praises of the Creator. In my overgrown garden silver beads of dew glistened in the sunlight, as they dripped from budding sycamore trees. Birds sang cheerfully while busily flitting to and fro with little twigs after the refreshing April shower. Today I was determined to plant something!

Carefully I opened the tiny packet of seeds and examined them. In small letters at the bottom of the packet I read: "Performance subject to growing conditions." Somehow it seemed wrong that these seeds had been trapped in a packet within the darkness of a drawer for so long. For them life could never begin - until they were planted! It was time to open a few drawers, let the sun shine in and do some 'spring cleaning.' I wondered, as I gazed at them, would it be possible that they would take root, survive and grow to maturity?

I thought about where I would plant them. Our country garden had never been landscaped, so that there were all types of terrain. Should I inadvertently drop some by 'the wayside,' there were numerous hungry birds waiting to snap them up before they ever got a chance to be grounded. 'Stony ground' was also in evidence, for although they would spring up rather quickly (because they had no depth) they would scorch in the sun and wither, being rootless. Thorns and weeds (I am ashamed to say) also abound in our garden. If I ignored the weeds and planted them there, it would be disastrous and they would be choked before they got a chance at all. Good ground, I am happy to say, does exist in our garden, and so … to work! I examined one tiny seed in the palm of my hand. How could something so insignificant grow into tall elegant flowers, and yet … it was possible! It reminded me of the grain of mustard seed that Jesus referred to in Matthew 13v31/32… "The kingdom of heaven is like to a grain of mustard seed, which a man took, and sowed in his field: Which indeed is the least of all seeds: but when it is grown, it is the greatest among herbs, and becometh a tree, so that the birds of the air come and lodge in the branches thereof." The seed referred to in previous verses of this chapter, however, represents the Word of God and the types of ground that it falls upon are like the categories of people in their respective responses to God's call upon their lives.

It is, indeed, a sobering thought to reflect upon which type of ground our lives represent. There are those who have allowed the devil to snatch the Word (as a bird devours seed) before it gets a chance to deepen and convict of sin. The seed falling into shallow stony ground reminds us of those who quickly receive the Word with joy, but when temptation, tribulation or persecutions arise, they become offended. Souls in the third category allow the Word to be choked by those 'thorny' areas of life: "the care of this world, the deceitfulness of riches" (Matthew 13v22), and "the pleasures of this life," and so they "bring no fruit to perfection" (Luke 8v14).

The good news is that just as God gave Adam and Eve free will in the beautiful Garden of Eden - we can choose to be good recipients of the 'seed,' or otherwise. His desire for us all is that we would be 'the good ground', for it is not His will "that any should perish, but that all should come to repentance" (2 Pet.3v9) and "grow in grace, and in the knowledge of our Lord and Saviour Jesus Christ." (2 Pet.3v18). This good productive ground brings forth fruit … "some an hundredfold, some sixtyfold, some thirtyfold." (Matthew 13v8). Note that some of us, as Christians, are less fruitful than others. But if we allow Him to 'weed and prune' our lives and 'be willing to be made willing' to rid them of even the tiniest 'weeds' - these lives of ours will abound in the 'fruits of the spirit': love, joy, peace, longsuffering, gentleness, goodness, faith, meekness, and temperance. (Galatians 5v22&23). The 'weeding' process may be a little painful, and perhaps humbling, but the results will be well worth it, both in this life and for eternity.

I remember one morning my young daughter came running to me. "Mum," she shouted, "what *are* these beautiful flowers?" Puzzled, I walked outdoors with her and looked towards where she pointed. It was then that I remembered! There amongst the grass and weeds grew a beautiful type of cultivated yellow and red gorse.

A year previously, I had absent-mindedly picked a very tiny sprig when out walking in a large public estate miles from where we lived. Upon our return home, I had again absent-mindedly inserted it in the soil, by the trees. Many months ago I had admired the beauty of the shrub and saw its potential for growth near my home. However, now I had to deal with the weeds that threatened to choke it! Not only are weeds a threat in the early stages of new life - but mature blooms are also very much at risk!

Like weeds, the things that threaten to choke us spiritually are not always easily discerned for the 'weeds' they are. Some seemingly harmless occupations may stunt our spiritual growth, and if *anything* in this life takes our mind off the Saviour, it must be uprooted, for the sake of our souls. We must be careful, though, not to harm the plant itself when weeding! The latter is a delicate process that must be accomplished with care and sensitivity. What better person to do the weeding, than the "Master Gardener" himself? When we allow *Him* to have full control of our lives, He makes no mistake! Something He will *never* do is to destroy us in the weeding process, for He loves us and wants the best conditions for each one of us. To uproot the plant with the weeds is akin to "throwing out the baby with the bath water!" Sometimes older, seemingly more 'mature' Christians, can stunt the growth of younger siblings in the Lord by their constant criticism and judgement. Exhortation will encourage growth, but constant severe judgement and criticism will inhibit it! "Judge not, that ye be not judged. For with what judgement ye judge, ye shall be judged: and with what measure ye mete, it shall be measured to you again. And why beholdest thou the mote that is in thy brother's eye, but considerest not the beam that is in thine own eye? Or how wilt thou say to thy brother, Let me pull out the mote out of thine eye; and, behold, a beam is in thine own eye? Thou hypocrite, first cast out the beam out of thine own eye; and then thou shalt see clearly to cast out the mote out of thy brother's eye." (Matt. 7v1-5)

How important it is too, to 'feed' that new growth. If I forget to water my houseplants, adding (just the right amount of) plant food, then the inevitable will happen! Sadly I have thrown away many a dead and shrivelled-up plant, all because it lacked that pure water which was necessary for its growth - yes, even survival. Because my mind was taken up with the cares of other things, I had neglected this basic, but essential duty. Once, I remember seeing one such poor plant and thinking: "perhaps it's not too late." Looking at it, I thought that only a miracle could raise it up! That night I watered the withered plant, and next morning those drooping leaves were renewed and looked decidedly healthier! However, this 'watering' must be a continual process - not a 'one-off wonder!' I recall those familiar instructions on many plants and shrubs... "Do not allow to dry out!" So it is, when we begin new life in Christ, we must be continually watered by the Word of God. In 1Peter 2v2 we read... "As newborn babes, desire the sincere milk of the word, that ye may grow thereby:" Jesus said: "He that rejecteth me, and receiveth not my words, hath one that judgeth him: the word that I have spoken, the same shall judge him in the last day." (John 12v48) If we are to be judged by His word, then surely it makes sense to read it?

"Ye shall know them by their fruits." (Matt. 7v16). Absent-minded people like me sometimes plant seeds, forgetting what it was they planted! But the ensuing bloom or fruit will show us *exactly* what it is... "Do men gather grapes, of thorns, or figs of thistles? Even so every good tree bringeth forth good fruit; but a corrupt tree bringeth forth evil fruit. A good tree cannot bring forth evil fruit, neither can a corrupt tree bring forth good fruit. Every tree that bringeth not forth good fruit is hewn down, and cast into the fire. Wherefore by their fruits ye shall know them." (Matt. 7v16-20)

Time and time again we may see the fruits, or otherwise, in the lives of individuals we know. That a tree which "bringeth not forth good fruit is hewn down, and cast into the fire," is a serious matter - but horrific in the light of a soul's destiny. As Christians, let us ever be aware, and discerning - not that we may stand in judgement, for (as we read in James 4v12)... "There is one lawgiver, who is able to save and to destroy: who art thou that judgest another?" Rather, let us use that discernment that we may pray effectively and fervently for the souls that Jesus died for.

Finally, what of that little packet of seeds? They reminded me of some tracts that I possessed - also in a drawer. Little seeds need to be sown, so that the miracle of new life can be made possible. As we have freely received - let us freely give. (Matthew 10v8). "He which soweth sparingly shall reap also sparingly; and he which soweth bountifully shall reap also bountifully." (2 Cor. 9v6). Always remember that some day you may be overjoyed to see an abundant and healthy bloom, somewhere that you would have least expected it! "Herein is my Father glorified, that ye bare much fruit; so shall ye be my disciples. As the Father hath loved me, so have I loved you: continue ye in my love." (John 15v8&9)

New Birth

We plant the seed, we hope, and pray...
And then one precious sun-filled day
We see a shoot, sweet promise of new life unfurled,
Triumphant from the death of this cold world.

A little garden in Co. Wicklow – the "garden of Ireland."

Here Today - and Gone Tomorrow
(1Peter 1v24&25)

(May 1st- May15th)

Its stunning beauty had dazzled me in the sunshine only days ago but now it was too late. The wind and rain had blown it hither and thither and I was annoyed with myself for not having taken that photograph. Now those once glorious pink petals lay there like abandoned dirty confetti, trampled underfoot by laughing students who made their way back to school after the bank holiday weekend.

What an interesting, challenging weekend that had been, but it had passed so quickly! The last thing on my mind was that I should capture the beauty of cherry blossom on camera... 'It will still be there,' I had thought. The bank holiday weekend had stretched tantalising ahead, although we had no plans to go anywhere. Just as well, because Saturday morning had brought some surprising news. My mother-in-law had sounded anxious and tired when I picked up the telephone. My father-in-law, I knew, had only recently been discharged from hospital after surgery. Was this what was wrong? "How are you?" I enquired. "Is everything ok?" His recovery, she had told me, was slow but sure - but apart from that, something else completely unexpected had happened... My husband's younger brother was leaving the monastery. "What!" I exclaimed, unable to take in the news.

"Yes," she said, "he's leaving this morning, but he doesn't want to return to us in the city. Not yet anyway. Would you take him in today?"

"Of course!" was my response, happy to be of assistance to her under the present difficult circumstances. I was very fond of my younger brother-in-law, and had been deeply concerned when he had decided to enter a monastery some months previously. It seemed like only yesterday that he had made this decision and ever since then he had been very much in our prayers...

My husband picked him up from the railway station that Saturday afternoon as arranged, and how good it was to see him after those eight months. While the rest of my family might complain about my culinary skills (or lack of them) now and then, he certainly didn't! "I haven't had meat in such a long time," he informed us, while hungrily clearing his plate... "Just fish, once a week on Fridays. I cooked it with turnips."

"Yuck," grimaced my eldest daughter.

"It must have been a very different way of life for you, I'm sure..." I remarked thoughtfully, my memories returning to a hot day, some years ago on the Greek Island of Crete. We had been standing in the courtyard of an old monastery, having viewed the horrific sight of the skulls of men, women and children who had been besieged there, and blown themselves up, rather than convert to Islam. 'What anguish and death can be caused by religion,' I thought, 'and how foolish were those Turkish invaders, to think that they could force someone to believe something. It is surely as foolish as thinking that we can force a tree to break out into blossom, or a bird to break out into song!' Only the gentle Saviour, knocking on the door of man's heart, can change that heart forever and fill it with joy and His love for others. But when a system of belief is based on rules and regulations, and even set prayers, it does not fill the heart of man with joy - and nor does it deal with the sin problem.

Long ago in 15th century Germany, there was a young man who was very successful academically - but greatly troubled about his soul. Thinking that he must work for his salvation, he entered a monastery. One day that monastery was visited by the Vicar General of all the Augustinian monasteries in Germany. This man could not help but notice this young monk, in particular, who stood out from all the rest. His sunken eyes and thin frame disclosed much fasting and sleep-depravation. When asked why he looked so sad, the young monk has been quoted as saying... "I don't know what will become of me. It is useless that I make vows to God, for sin is still the strongest thing in me." One day, years later, as that young monk sat in his cell studying the New Testament, he read: "For therein is the righteousness of God revealed from faith to faith: as it is written, *The just shall live by faith*." (Rom. 1v17). And so, it came to pass that wondrous light penetrated that little cell, and a searching soul was saved by grace through faith. How marvellous that God had preserved His Word throughout the dark ages and that Martin Luther

(1483-1546), touched by that immortal Word, was tremendously used of God throughout Europe, and indeed the entire world.

I recall a tiny old lady, all in black, toothless and with only one arm, walking in the courtyard of the old Greek Orthodox monastery. In the heat of the day, we had entered the cool shadows of the old church, and my husband had sat down on a very ornate antique chair. The old lady, on seeing this, rushed towards him and with wild gesticulations and raised voice indicated that he should *never ever* sit on *that* chair. My husband, of course, apologetically got out of the 'special' chair and I smiled at the old lady, wanting so much to communicate with her - to tell her of God's love for her and that, in the light of eternity, these things do not matter. I have often thought about her and prayed that somehow, as with Martin Luther, the truth of God's Word would penetrate her very soul - like those rays of light shining through the bars of the high windows of the monastery... Surely "Thy word is a lamp unto my feet, and a light unto my path." (Psalm 119v105).

Later, I found my husband having a heated discussion with one of the elderly monks, who spoke perfect English. A duel was being fought between the Word of God and man's traditions and philosophies. Yes, our transient lives (like the cherry blossom) bloom for a little while, and then die in this scene of time but oh that we would be... "born again, not of corruptible seed, but of incorruptible, by the word of God, which liveth and abideth for ever." (1Pet. 1v23).

We may attempt to, but we cannot win, an argument with God's Word. Books may come and go, cults may rise and wane, but throughout the ages the Word of God stands triumphant, and infallible. It is one of the vital pieces of armour in the Christian's life, all of which is described in Eph. 6v10-18... "And take the helmet of salvation, and the *sword of the Spirit, which is the word of God;*" (verse 17). Throughout history, the devil has tried, by various devious means, to dispense with God's Word. "Yea, hath God said...?" he questioned Eve in the Garden of Eden. (Gen.3v1)

People have twisted God's Word and re-written the Bible to accommodate their own desires, or wrongly-held beliefs. However, they do this to their own destruction, for we read in Rev. 22v18&19... "For I testify unto every man that heareth the words of the prophecy of this book, if any man should add unto these things, God shall add unto him the plagues that are written in this book: And if any man shall take away from the words of the book of this prophecy, God shall take away his part out of the book of life, and out of the holy city, and from the things which are written in this book."

For those who love the Saviour, the Word of God is their Guide Book throughout life's journey. When times are turbulent, we can immerse ourselves in its comforting words, promises and loving reassurance; yet it also exhorts and rebukes us as necessary. To the unregenerate it is, at best, a beautiful piece of literature - but to those who have made the Lord their Captain in the changing scenes of life, it is exceedingly more. It is everything to them, and they love it - even enough to die for its very survival... "And I saw thrones, and they sat upon them, and judgement was given unto them; and I saw the souls of them that were beheaded for the witness of Jesus, and *for the word of God*, and which had not worshipped the beast, neither his image, neither had received his mark upon their foreheads, or in their hands; and they lived and reigned with Christ a thousand years." (Rev.20v4).

A thousand years! What an incredibly long span of time it appears to us, especially when we compare it with the average person's lifetime, but in Psalm 90v4 we see the Lord's view on a thousand years... "For a thousand years in thy sight are but as yesterday when it is past, and as a watch in the night." I recall standing by the graveside of an aunt of mine and as I stood there reflecting upon the life of the deceased, another aunt said: "You know, life is just like this..." She rapidly blew a puff of air, and waved her hand from left to right. How apt are the words of Psalm 103v14-19: "For he knoweth our frame; he remembereth that we are dust. As for man, his days are as grass: as a flower of the field, so he flourisheth. For the wind passeth over it, and it is gone; and the place thereof shall know it no more. But the mercy of the Lord is from everlasting to everlasting upon them that fear him, and his righteousness unto children's children; To such as keep his covenant, and to those that remember his commandments to do them. The Lord hath prepared his throne in the heavens; and his kingdom ruleth over all."

'Yes,' I thought, as I sat now, years later at dinner with my brother-in-law. 'How rapidly a life can change course – either for good or evil!' Often, too, those positive changes can come about as the Lord responds to our earnest prayer. As for the cherry blossom, it had vanished over a weekend with the harsh wind and rain, and nothing remained of its beauty and glory. We live out our fragile lives, not knowing what tomorrow may hold. Like a Greek monastery, perched high on the cliff-edge of mountainous terrain, we are closer to the precipice of eternity than we think. Let us then search for the truth in His abiding Word - for if we seek, we shall find. (Matt. 7v7). "Search the scriptures," Jesus tells us in John 5v39, "for in them ye think ye have eternal life: and they are they which testify of me."

"I am come a light into the world, that whosoever believeth on me should not abide in darkness." (John 12v46) How wrong it is to substitute the teachings and traditions of man for the Word of God! "And if any man hear my words, and believe not, I judge him not: for I came not to judge the world, but to save the world. He that rejecteth me, and receiveth not my words, hath one that judgeth him: the word that I have spoken, the same shall judge him in the last day." (John 12v47&48). Clearly there is only one way to find out the words that Jesus has spoken. We must read, and search the scriptures - those scriptures for which men were burned in the flames of persecution.

"All scripture," we learn in 2Tim. 3v16&17, "is given by inspiration of God, and is profitable for doctrine, for reproof, for correction, for instruction in righteousness; That the man of God may be perfect, throughly furnished unto all good works." As a young Christian, I was advised to start my reading of the Bible in the New Testament, and I believe that this is good advice. Remembering the short life span of the cherry blossom, and indeed, our own earthly bodies, I compare both with the Word of God - which is as beautiful and relevant today, as it was thousands of years ago.

My young brother-in-law's lifestyle had changed radically, in the space of one week. A few days after he had come to stay with us, he had read a newspaper and spotted an interesting job. Next day he returned home to his family and applied for this job - and a day later he was called for interview, at which he was offered a position to start on Monday morning. The circumstances of our lives may change even today but if we live for the things that are eternal, we have nothing to fear, neither in this life or the life to come. The Lord wants, above all, to plant His vital seed within our hearts, so that "this mortal put on immortality." (1Cor. 15v53). What do our lives consist of? Of course we must live, and work and go about our business in this world. Indeed, nowhere in God's Word, are we asked to shut ourselves away from the outside world; there are no examples in the Bible of God's servants being "forbidden to marry," or living a monastic or convent life. It is in 1Tim. 4v1-3, that we learn of this matter: "Now the Spirit speaketh expressly, that in the latter times some shall depart from the faith, giving heed to seducing spirits, and doctrines of devils; Speaking lies in hypocrisy; having their conscience seared with a hot iron; Forbidding to marry, and commanding to abstain from meats, which God hath created to be received with thanksgiving of them which believe and know the truth." However, as we live and work in this world - do we know, and acknowledge Jesus as Saviour and Lord of these lives of ours? "Go to now, ye that say, Today or to morrow we will go into such a city, and continue there a year, and buy and sell and get gain: Whereas ye know not what shall be on the morrow. For what is your life? It is even a vapour, that appeareth for a little time, and then vanisheth away." (James 4v13&14)

In our brief lives, which are but a vapour in the light of eternity, let us give Him the precedence in all things, forsaking short-term glory - for a home in heaven. "By faith Moses, when he was come to years, refused to be called the son of Pharaoh's daughter; Choosing rather to suffer affliction with the people of God, than to enjoy the pleasures of sin for a season; Esteeming the reproach of Christ greater riches than the treasures of Egypt: for he had respect unto the recompence of the reward." (Heb. 11v24-26)

If we obey, by faith, as Moses did, and as Abraham did... "Seeing the promises afar off," (Heb. 11v13), we too shall some day leave these corruptible bodies, "to be with Christ which is far better." (Phil. 1v23). He can change you now, in the "twinkling of an eye," to be the person He wants you to be, and then some wonderful day these glorious promises will be fulfilled... "Behold I shew you a mystery; We shall not all sleep, but we shall all be changed, In a moment, in the twinkling of an eye, at the last trump: for the trumpet shall sound, and the dead shall be raised incorruptible, and we shall all be changed. For this corruptible must put on incorruption, and this mortal must put on immortality. So when this corruptible shall have put on incorruption, and this mortal shall have put on immortality, then shall be brought to pass the saying that is written, Death is swallowed up in victory. O death, where is thy sting? O grave, where is thy victory? The sting of death is sin; and the strength of sin is the law. *But thanks be to God, which giveth us the victory through our Lord Jesus Christ."* (*1Cor. 15v51-57*).

Here today and gone tomorrow,
A life of joy, or hidden sorrow,
But if we choose to serve the King -
In Heaven's courts we'll ever sing!

A lovely Cherry Blossom Tree - just before the blossom falls!

(10)

A Faithful Friend - And the God of All Comfort
(2Cor. 12v9& 2Cor. 1v3)

(May 16th – May 31st)

The bedroom ceiling appeared to whirl around in circles, furniture moved before my eyes and I felt extremely sick. Even when I closed my eyes, there was constant movement in the darkness. Then I felt as though I was going to lose consciousness and a terrible thirst overwhelmed me. "Please help me... I need water!" I tried to shout but the words came weakly. Would they hear me above the sound of the radio? "Here Mum." My youngest daughter was approaching with a long glass of cold water. What a welcome sight! I drank it all quickly, and then she filled it up again. "Thanks love," I said, "I feel much better. Would you help me to get the dinner?" I tried to stand up, but the dizzy sensation returned, and I reluctantly collapsed unto the bed again. "What on *earth* is wrong with me," I muttered, "after two weeks of this, I should be starting to feel better. I feel sea-sick, but I'm not at sea!"
"You shouldn't walk around Mum. We'll manage. Just stay where you are for the moment." I nodded in silent reluctance.

Alone with my thoughts once more, I remembered the events of a certain sunny afternoon, some weeks previously. As I had gone about the usual school runs that day, I had noticed him on a few occasions, on roads close to our home. He looked dejected, hungry and abandoned. 'Poor thing,' I had thought, as I drove past, 'I wonder who owns him? Someone's probably thrown him out. Aren't people awful? I hope he doesn't get knocked down - or picked up by the pound.' Then, on the final run home, my youngest daughter spotted him, lying only yards from our home. At first I thought that he was dead. He lay by the side of the road, tongue hanging out, gasping, and his ribs protruding through his matted, unkempt coat. We managed somehow to get him into the garden. He was thirsty and hungry beyond belief. Bread, potatoes, vegetables, long drinks of water and milk, and even tins of cat food were devoured by him in a matter of minutes! (We have never owned a dog - just several cats, a hamster and two goldfish - hence the lack of dog food!) I was amazed when he ran off with a tin of cat food in his mouth, and managed to partially rip it open with his bare teeth. Biting viciously and hungrily through the metal, blood poured from his gums and mouth, and my daughter screamed. Our five cats weren't impressed either. I managed to extract the tin from his mouth, offering him some water to drink in order to clean his wounds. Then he noticed me carrying groceries in from the car. Grabbing a six-pack of potato crisps in his teeth, he ran away and proceeded to burst open three of them, devouring the contents almost as fast as you can say "walkies!" Yes, 'Mr. Shaggy Dog' played havoc with our lives for just over a week and yet I grew very fond of him.

Because the cats (one of them ill and elderly) were terrified of him, I had to find a home for him. As a consequence of my advertisement, a family called the next Saturday and offered him a good home. With relief, and yet sadness, I said my 'goodbyes.' I had been praying for the right person, or people, to adopt him; I believe that the Lord hears all our requests - even those which may appear trivial. "Be careful for nothing; but in everything by prayer and supplication with thanksgiving let your requests be made known unto God." (Phil. 4v6). How essential it is to remember that *thanksgiving* in answer to our prayers. In Luke 17v11-19, we can read an account of how Jesus healed ten lepers, but only *one* returned to glorify God and to give thanks. (Luke 17v15&16). "And Jesus answering said, Were there not ten cleansed? But where *are* the nine?" (Verse17). As I gave the father of the family a little tract, I told him how the Lord had answered my prayers. Smiling, he accepted it, and then told me that this was the first day out for his three young children, after being sick for quite a while. "They're enjoying the drive out into the country," he said, "It's a beautiful day!"

A couple of weeks later, as I struggled to get to my feet feeling thoroughly sick, I wondered… 'Now, did I catch this virus from those children - I *was* in very close contact with them, while they were here…' Children very often 'bounce back' after an illness, but adults and older people in general, take much longer to recover. Alarmed at my increasing lack of balance I consulted a doctor, although it was after surgery hours. "It sounds to me like vertigo," He informed me, "something very common in the aftermath of a viral infection. You need time to rest and recover, and please, *no* driving. It's much too dangerous." Thanking him, I set the phone down, feeling relieved. Well, at least it wasn't some mysterious, deadly disease... but oh no! How were the children to get to their schools, given the lack of public transport to the latter? 'But of course,' I thought, 'I must pray.' If the Lord can provide a loving home for a scruffy little mongrel, then He can make me well enough to get on the road again!' I must confess that I am not a very good patient! As someone who has been blessed with good health over the years, I have found it very depressing on the occasions when I have felt weak or ill. However, I believe that these times are valuable, in that they present great opportunities for spiritual growth, and they show us just how fragile and dependant upon the Lord we are. "I will praise thee; for I am fearfully and wonderfully made: marvellous are thy works; and that my soul knoweth right well. My substance was not hid from thee, when I was made in secret, and curiously wrought in the lowest parts of the earth. Thine eyes did see my substance, yet being unperfect; and in thy book all my members were written, which in continuance were fashioned, when as yet there was none of them." (Psalm 139v14-16).

Still downcast, weary and unwell, one morning I read these words... "And he said unto me, My grace is sufficient for thee; for my strength is made perfect in weakness. Most gladly therefore will I rather glory in my infirmities, that the power of Christ may rest upon me. Therefore I take pleasure in infirmities, in reproaches, in necessities, in persecutions, in distresses for Christ's sake: for when I am weak, then am I strong." (2Cor. 12v9&10). Slowly but surely I began to feel better, and then I heard of someone else who had similar symptoms. "She has all my sympathy," I said. Surely, if we have suffered (albeit temporarily) then we are in a better position to offer our sincere compassion and comforting words of encouragement to others? Paul, in 2Cor. 1v3&4, tells the Corinthians... "Blessed be God, even the Father of our Lord Jesus Christ, the Father of mercies, and the God of all comfort; Who comforteth us in all our tribulation, that we may be able to comfort them which are in any trouble by the comfort wherewith we ourselves are comforted of God." I had learned too, that I was not 'made of steel' - some sort of self-sufficient 'super Mum' at the 'beck and call' of everyone. Often, being really sick may reduce us to tears, but we are drawn closer to that Faithful Friend who cares for us more than anyone else in the world.

Several things happened around that time, which all contributed to my feelings of despondency. "Terrible weather for May," commented a neighbour, as we both looked up at the grey sky, just bursting to rain again. Then one dark rainy Monday evening, I heard some shocking news. The telephone rang, and my mother sounded anxious. "Is everyone alright? There's been an awful bus accident down your way." Reassuring her that we were fine, I listened to the news bulletin. Five young girls around the age range of my three daughters had lost their lives in this accident, and many more were injured. I couldn't bear to think about it and sat down on the edge of my bed to cry. Why did this awful thing have to happen? They had their whole lives before them... As I sat there, I felt the Lord's comforting presence surround me, as I have on other occasions when I have most needed Him. Somehow, that viral infection (which still lingered a little); that nearby tragic accident; the awful weather; my husband's increasing problems with diabetes; irritable teenagers studying for exams; and the subsequent death of the elderly pet all contributed to the way I felt. Yet I know that I had very little to be despondent about, personally, when I considered what others had to endure. Surely I should be rejoicing - not feeling sorry for myself? Yes, time and time again I have felt the loving arms of "the God of all comfort." How good it was to know Him! 'How would I react if a terrible tragedy (such as that bus accident) came to my door?' I thought. Yes, I would be devastated, life would never be the same again; yet my sovereign God in whom I trust would have to carry me throughout life's journey... otherwise how would I survive? "For we have not an high priest which cannot be touched with the feeling of our infirmities; but was in all points tempted like as we are, yet without sin. Let us therefore come boldly unto the throne of grace, that we may obtain mercy, and find grace to help in time of need." (Heb. 4v15&16).

We all at times in our lives, have felt low - perhaps physically (because of various degrees of ill health), perhaps psychologically, or even spiritually. However, in 1Thess. 5v16&17 the Christian is exhorted to: "Rejoice evermore. Pray without ceasing," and of course it is not a sin to weep - for "Jesus wept." (John 11v35). Like David, the Psalmist, we can pour out our hearts to Someone who really cares. Though no one else in the world will hear our cry - *He* certainly will. "Give ear to my prayer, O God; and hide not thyself from my supplication. Attend unto me, and hear me: I mourn in my complaint, and make a noise; Because of the voice of the enemy, because of the oppression of the wicked: for they cast iniquity upon me, and in wrath they hate me. My heart is sore pained within me: and the terrors of death are fallen upon me. Fearfulness and trembling are come upon me, and horror hath overwhelmed me. And I said, Oh that I had wings like a dove! For then would I fly away, and be at rest." (Psalm 55v1-6). What I find encouraging about the Psalms is the fact that, although they may start with a cry of anguish, most of them conclude on a note of optimism. The few Psalms that *don't* end on this note will lead us on to triumph in a subsequent Psalm. This particular Psalm concludes… "Cast thy burden upon the Lord, and he shall sustain thee: he shall never suffer the righteous to be moved. But thou O God, shalt bring them down into the pit of destruction: bloody and deceitful men shall not live out half their days; but I will trust in thee." (Psalm 55v22&23).

Scarcely any individual would feel that they were able for the terrible events that beset Job in his life. Nevertheless, his story too, like those Psalms of David, concluded victoriously. Like David, he would ultimately cry… "Yea, though I walk through the valley of the shadow of death, I will fear no evil: for thou art with me; thy rod and thy staff they comfort me. Thou preparest a table before me in the presence of mine enemies: thou annointest my head with oil; my cup runneth over. Surely goodness and mercy shall follow me all the days of my life: and I will dwell in the house of the Lord for ever." (Psalm 23v4-6). Job lost his health; his loved ones, his wealth - and the respect of those who were once his friends. "All my inward friends abhorred me: and they whom I loved are turned against me. My bone cleaveth to my skin and to my flesh, and I am escaped with the skin of my teeth." (Job 19v19&20). Compare these words, however, with those written towards the end of the story… "And the Lord turned the captivity of Job, when he prayed for his friends: also the Lord gave Job twice as much as he had before." (Job 42v10). "So the Lord blessed the latter end of Job more than his beginning: for he had fourteen thousand sheep, and six thousand camels, and a thousand yoke of oxen, and a thousand she asses. He had also seven sons and three daughters. And he called the name of the first Je-mi-ma; and the name of the second, Ke-zi-a; and the name of the third, Ker-en-hap-puch. And in all the land were no women found so fair as the daughters of Job: and their father gave them inheritance among their brethren. After this lived Job an hundred and forty years, and saw his sons, and his sons' sons, even four generations. So Job died, being old and full of days." (Job 42v12-17).

Restored in health, I took a walk one mild evening with my husband who was also feeling somewhat better. I was joyful in my spirit, as I absorbed the fresh air, and the smell of pink and white blossom that cloaked the May hedgerows. I appreciated the health that, all too often, I had previously taken for granted, and had a fresh understanding and much more compassion for those who were feeling unwell. All too often we fail to recognise the private grief or depression that lies behind a well-dressed and seemingly cheerful exterior. But God sees it all… "for his eye seeth every precious thing." (Job 28v10). The Lord tells Samuel in 1Sam. 16v7… "Look not on his countenance, or on the height of his stature; because I have refused him: for the Lord seeth not as man seeth; for man looketh on the outward appearance, but the Lord looketh on the heart." I watched with interest as little girls with costly 'first communion dresses' made their way to a local church - a common sight in May. Some, however, were more poorly dressed than others - but this means nothing to the Lord, either way. "For in Christ Jesus neither circumcision availeth any thing, nor uncircumcision, but a new creature." (Gal. 6v15). He sees into the very heart and soul - and He knows our every thought and intent. His eyes still look with compassion upon the inhabitants of this earth, just as they did thousands of years ago. He saw Hagar, alone with her child Ishmael, ready to die of thirst in the desert. "What aileth thee Hagar? Fear not; for God hath heard the voice of the lad where he is. Arise, lift up the lad, and hold him in thine hand; for I will make him a great nation. And God opened her eyes, and she saw a well of water; and she went, and filled the bottle with water, and gave the lad drink."

(Gen. 21v17-19). He knows when a little sparrow falls to the ground (Matt. 10v29) and I believe that he knows every single occurrence throughout the world (however minuscule in our eyes). I believe that He even had compassion upon the dejected and starving animal that we found that day; for He brought him to our door, and found him a home. How much more then, does His caring eye look with compassion upon the sons and daughters of man, whom He has made in His own image, and for whom He sent His only Son to die?

Because we live in a tainted world we will most probably, at some time or other, be subject to some sort of heartache or illness. Perhaps at times we may even feel like a modern day Job. But we have a 'Burden-Bearer!' "That it might be fulfilled which was spoken by E-sai-as the prophet, saying, Himself took our infirmities, and bare our sicknesses." (Matt. 8v17). Our sorrows are His sorrows, our burdens are His and if we make the eternal God our refuge and trust Him for tomorrow - our latter end (like that of Job) shall be blessed forevermore. "Oh that my words were now written! Oh that they were printed in a book! That they were graven with an iron pen and laid in the rock for ever!" (Job 19v23&24). And so, the Lord answered Job's cry from the heart. His words of anguish *were* printed in a book, for they were printed in God's Word which is still read by people today - and will be forevermore, for "the word of the Lord endureth for ever..." (1Pet. 1v25). Surely His Word is even more permanent than those "graven with an iron pen and lead in the rock for ever!" Job's beautiful words in verses 25 and 26 of Chapter 19 are prophetic, referring to Jesus his Saviour... "For I know that my redeemer liveth, and that he shall stand at the latter day upon the earth: And though after my skin worms destroy this body, yet in my flesh shall I see God..."

Today Job is rejoicing in the Kingdom of Heaven, but the record of his tribulation upon this earth lives on in the Word of God as an inspiration and an encouragement to those of us still walking life's twisting highway. James in his epistle says... "Take, my brethren, the prophets who have spoken in the name of the Lord, for an example of suffering affliction, and of patience. Behold, we count them happy which endure. Ye have heard of the patience of Job, and have seen the end of the Lord; that the Lord is very pitiful, and of tender mercy." (James 5v10&11). Therefore "We are troubled on every side, yet not distressed; we are perplexed, but not in despair; Persecuted, but not forsaken; cast down but not destroyed; Always bearing about in the body the dying of the Lord Jesus, that the life also of Jesus might be made manifest in our body." (2Cor. 4v8-10).

Around the time that I was feeling unwell, I remember being appalled by news of a documentary on conditions in an old people's home, not far from our locality. Naturally we may fear what the future holds for us when we are vulnerable elderly people, but if we have made the God of Abraham, Isaac, Jacob, David and Job, *our* God, then *what* have we to fear? Just as the Lord was with David in his dual with Goliath, He is able to vanquish the "giants" of pain, illness or despair in *our* lives. For He... "who forgiveth all thine iniquities; who healeth all thy diseases;" lives to... "satisfy thy mouth with good things; so that thy youth is renewed like the eagle's." (See Psalm 103v1-5). Better, by far, than any insurance policy or 'sheltered housing,' is to know that Friend who "loveth at all times," (Prov.17v17) - and to rest in the loving arms of the "God of all comfort"... "Who delivered us from so great a death, and doth deliver: in whom we trust that he will yet deliver us..." (2Cor. 1v10).

Look Up!
When you are despondent
Do not dwell upon the loss,
Look ever unto Jesus
And cling to the cross.
When all around
Seems bleak as darkest night -
Look beyond the clouds
For that eternal Light.
This world's pain and glory
Will soon pass away,
From the black of midnight
To the dawn of Heaven's Day,
And though you are oppressed
By sin on every side,
Look upon that face of Love,
For His grace will provide.

"He cutteth out rivers among the rocks and his eye seeth every precious thing."
(Job 28v10)

(11)

Praying in the Glen - With Forgiveness in my Heart
(Mark 11v25&26)

(June 1st – June 15$^{th)}$

There is a beautiful glen to which I sometimes walk, when I wish to be close to the Lord. Always I am reminded of Psalm 104, when reflecting on this peaceful, inspiring place. "My meditation of him shall be sweet: I will be glad in the Lord." (Verse 34) Nature at its best is on display here, and I hope and pray that it will remain so, as long as there is a soul left upon the earth to appreciate it! "He sendeth the springs into the valleys, which run among the hills. They give drink to every beast of the field: the wild asses quench their thirst. By them shall the fowls of the heaven have their habitation, which sing among the branches." (Psalm 104v10-12). Trees and gorse, yellow-blossomed for much of the year, grace the surrounding hills, and far beyond I can glimpse the blue sea against the horizon. "O Lord, how manifold are thy works! In wisdom hast thou made them all: the earth is full of thy riches. So is this great and wide sea, wherein are things creeping innumerable, both small and great beasts." (Psalm 104v24&25). Apart from distant farmhouses and their barns, no evidence of modern development disturbs the beauty of the area.

Cattle graze in the emerald grass, fox cubs play in the little forest, squirrels scurry amongst its trees and unusual birdsong fills the valley. "The trees of the Lord are full of sap; the cedars of Lebanon, which he hath planted; Where the birds make their nests: as for the stork, the fir trees are her house." (Psalm 104v16&17). Today, as I write, is one of those gloriously warm summer days that always seem to occur during exam week. I smile at that memory - glad that I have long since finished with this 'millstone of youth.' It is June, the whin blossom is waning, but nature has taken over and the trees are in their splendour of full leaf.

Today I have come here to pray and to reflect on forgiveness, for this is something which has troubled my heart recently. The warmth of the sun embraces me, reminding me of God's love, and of that exhortation in Ephesians 4v31&32… "Let all bitterness, and wrath, and anger, and clamour, and evil speaking, be put away from you, with all malice: And be ye kind one to another, tenderhearted, forgiving one another, even as God for Christ's sake hath forgiven you." I thank Him for my life, my health, the gift of sight which He has given me to appreciate His creation - and most of all for His great salvation, which is outlined in those well-known verses of John 3v16&17… "For God so loved the world, that he gave his only begotten Son, that whosoever believeth in him should not perish, but have everlasting life. For God sent not his Son into the world to condemn the world; but that the world through him might be saved." I am totally alone with Him, and I thank Him for this opportunity. As I sit silently on my jacket upon the grass (which is still a little dewy from last night) I spot some cattle grazing lower in the valley. "For every beast of the forest is mine, and the cattle upon a thousand hills." (Psalm 50v10). They don't see me, and hopefully there isn't a bull amongst them! A bumblebee drones lazily past, and a little rabbit hops out from the gorse. "The high hills are a refuge for the wild goats; and the rocks for the conies." (Psalm 104v18) Unaware of my presence, it nibbles in the grass, but with slight movement on my part, it nervously looks up, its beautiful eyes wide with fear. Swiftly it runs to safety, that labyrinth of little secret passages on the hillside, which is 'home'.

I too, feel at home, at peace with these the innocent members of God's creation. Unlike mankind, they have no sin - although they have been greatly affected by the consequences of sin. They bear no grudges, and if they attack it is for the purpose of self defence, survival, or for basic reasons of hunger or fear. The human race, in contrast, can attack (not just physically) but with their tongues - those little 'members' referred to in James chapter 3 can leave deeper wounds than a knife! In verses 6-8 we read: "And the tongue is a fire, a world of iniquity: so is the tongue among our members, that it defileth the whole body, and setteth on fire the course of nature; and it is set on fire of hell. For every kind of beasts, and of birds, and of serpents, and of things in the sea, is tamed, and hath been tamed of mankind: But the tongue can no man tame; it is an unruly evil, full of deadly poison." Yes it is true that "the tongue can no man tame," but *God* can! "Now the God of peace, that brought again from the dead our Lord Jesus, that great shepherd of the sheep, through the blood of the everlasting covenant, Make you perfect in every good work to do his will, working in you that which is wellpleasing in his sight, through Jesus Christ; to whom be glory for ever and ever. Amen." (Hebrews 13v20&21)

No one understands the darker side of human nature *more* than Jesus. Physically and emotionally bruised after all the loving and miraculous things he had done, His short earthly life culminated in being unjustly accused and nailed to a Roman cross. To feel hurt, and the pain of rejection or to ask 'why?' is not in itself sinful, for Jesus cried out: "My God, my God, why hast thou forsaken me?" (Matt. 27v46). However, my hurt must never be all-consuming, until it reaches that point where bitterness takes over, and I cannot pray for the person or people involved, with love in my heart.

Indeed, it is only love, the greatest of all attributes (as we learn in 1Cor. 13) which will carry me through - for love never fails. Whatever happens to me, and however unfairly I think I have been treated, my response must always be Christ-like. In Matthew 5v38&39, He tells me: "Ye have heard that it hath been said, An eye for an eye, and a tooth for a tooth: But I say unto you, That ye resist not evil: but whosoever shall smite thee on thy right cheek, turn to him the other also."

It is important to remember, at this point, that if I am walking close to the Lord, then persecution is inevitable at some time and in some form. In 2Tim. 3v12, I learn that "all that will live godly in Christ Jesus shall suffer persecution." Sadly, the latter may even be perpetrated by those who profess to be Christians. Nevertheless, whatever the source of the persecution, I must love and pray for those that 'despitefully use' me.

Above all, I must not let anyone destroy my peace with the Lord. "Because iniquity shall abound, the love of many shall wax cold. But he that shall endure unto the end, the same shall be saved," we are told in Matthew 24v12&13. The signs of those end days are described throughout this chapter, but whatever I am to face in days to come - I can do so in the strength of my Redeemer, whose "merciful kindness is great towards us, and whose truth endureth forever." (Psalm 117v2).

As He has forgiven me, so I must learn to forgive others. If they do not respond to this, I can only continue to pray and to love them - even in the face of persecution. "For if ye love them which love you, what reward have ye? Do not even the publicans the same?" asks Jesus in Matthew 5v46. "And when ye stand praying, forgive, if ye have ought against any: that your Father also which is in heaven may forgive you your trespasses. But if ye do not forgive, neither will your Father which is in heaven forgive your trespasses." (Mark 11v25&26). The matter is clear: if I do not forgive, I am not forgiven and this is a very serious position for the Christian. Neither can I "render evil for evil" (1Pet.3v9) for "vengeance is mine; I will repay, saith the Lord." (Romans 12v19).

Some day justice will be done, and "wrong shall be ended when Jesus is King," is a line from C.S. Horne's lovely old hymn "Sing we the King who is coming to reign." Meanwhile, "I will lift up mine eyes unto the hills, from whence cometh my help. My help cometh from the Lord, which made heaven and earth." (Psalm 121v1&2). Just now I look up to the sky above, and then beyond to the distant Irish sea, so deep and blue, and my thoughts return once more to Psalm 104 - that lovely Psalm of nature. "Bless the Lord, O my soul, O Lord my God, thou art very great; thou art clothed with honour and majesty. Who coverest thyself with light as with a garment: who stretchest out the heavens like a curtain: Who layeth the beams of His chambers in the waters: who maketh the clouds His chariot: who walketh upon the wings of the wind:" (Psalm 104v1-3).

This same great God, the Creator of highest heaven and deepest sea, is He who "as far as the east is from the west, so far hath He removed our transgressions from us." (Psalm 103v12). In the light of His great mercy towards me, I must now (in His mighty strength) pray for those who have trespassed against me, and I must do so with love and forgiveness in my heart ... for thine, O Lord "is the kingdom, and the power, and the glory, for ever. Amen." (Matthew 6v13).

O Lord, Creator of earth and sky,
Who sent thy Son for me to die,
Assist me to forgive, I pray,
And fill me with thy love today.

In the glens of Antrim: in the distance a misty sea blends with the
sky.

(12)

A Winter's Day in Summer
2Cor. 4v15-18)

(June 16th - June 30^{th)}

My youngest daughter had just finished school for that year, and along with her sisters, we were looking forward to the long summer holidays that lay ahead. It was Saturday morning and I was wearily resting after a stressful week. My bedroom curtains remained drawn as I was fully aware of the swollen grey skies and undesirable weather conditions without. I sighed, turned over again, and dozily dreamed of warm blue seas and laughter on some distant Mediterranean beach...

This pleasant reverie was somewhat abruptly interrupted by my husband bursting into the dark bedroom. Unlike me, he's a 'morning person.' Up with the rising sun (which didn't seem to rise that morning) and as practical as ever, he was informing me of something else I would have preferred not to have known ... "You'll never guess what's happened ... The oil has run done. I wondered why the Aga had gone out. We should have checked it this week - I didn't realise it was so low. It's cold this morning too, and more heavy rain is forecast for the whole day."

I sighed, feeling more dejected by the minute. "O.k. I'll ring the company and see if they'll deliver today - although something tells me that they don't do so at weekends," I added pessimistically. I tried to bury my head in the Mediterranean sand again, but somehow the dream wouldn't come back. Outside the monotonous drip of the rain from the spouting informed me that, like it or not, this was Ireland - and a cold rainy summer's day in Ireland at that!

After numerous telephone calls, I decided that I was right about weekend deliveries. Defiantly I pulled on some bright summer clothes, but then, in shivering acknowledgement of reality, reached for a woolly cardigan. After breakfast I was feeling more optimistic - but even more so after reading a portion of the scriptures ... "For all things are for your sakes, that the abundant grace might through the thanksgiving of many redound to the glory of God. For which cause we faint not; but though our outward man perish, yet the inward man is renewed day by day. For our light affliction, which is but for a moment, worketh for us a far more exceeding and eternal weight of glory; While we look not at the things which are seen, but at the things which are not seen: for the things which are seen are temporal: but the things which are not seen are eternal." (2 Cor. 4v15-18). Yes, the Christian can be optimistic under all circumstances, providing he or she accepts that the Lord is in control, teaching us important lessons through our temporary inconveniences. If we learn from these, we will appreciate all that He has given us, grow in grace and patience and learn to give Him the glory in all situations. In my case this is "easier said than done!"

How selfish I felt for letting weather conditions get the better of me. I thought of others in worse situations than us, for although we lived in (and enjoyed) the beauty of the countryside, we were not dependent upon the fruits of the land for our income. However, I thought of the mildew and blight which would affect crops in this persistent rain … Ultimately agriculture, the oldest occupation in the world, is also the most vital, at the very roots of society and crucial to the well-being of all mankind.

As the gloomy day wore on, the electricity failed while I was preparing dinner. Now we had no cooking facilities and no water, as the pump to our well is dependant on electricity and we are not on a mains supply. This tiny inconvenience involving basic hygiene (washing/flushing toilets etc.) and lack of cooking facilities affected us for hours and yet, to me, it seemed interminable and really awful. 'How must others in Third World societies cope with these problems on a daily basis?' I thought. "Mum!" shouted my daughters; "we're hungry." Without delay I jumped into the car and headed towards the village, where I knew there would be a visiting fast-food van on a Saturday evening. As I drove, I felt rumbling, gnawing hunger pangs - an unusual feeling for anyone in our society today - unless they are on a weight- reducing diet! 'Real and constant hunger pain must be truly awful,' I thought, as I drove. At least I knew that I had access to food, be it far from 'cordon bleu!' Some cold meat and salad ingredients, along with the chips completed my purchases, and soon I was home, where the children had lit a fire. After tucking in hungrily, we sat watching the flames licking around the turf, in the fading light of another day. My husband, who had been trying to do some outdoor work, had been constantly hampered by outbreaks of heavy rain. "This is ridiculous," I said. "Here we are in July, warming ourselves by a fire like it was darkest winter." Then, feeling ashamed of my selfish outburst - I remembered those hunger pangs. "Well, at least we have food and shelter," I whispered, "and most of all I know the Provider of these things and can get to know Him better, because of His long-suffering towards us." (Romans 2v4). It was time to count my blessings, and thank God for them!

Just then the fridge/freezer, dishwasher, washing machine and lights all swung into action again, while in the attic I could hear a surge of water filling the empty tank - and above all of these welcome sounds rose a cheer from the family. Outside a pale setting sun emerged from a great cloud and the faintest hint of a rainbow could be seen on a far-away green hill. Somehow I had learned something from this "grey day," and the words of Psalm 68v19 took on a whole new meaning... "Blessed be the Lord, who daily loadeth us with benefits, even the God of our salvation. Se-lah."

The volatile nature of Irish weather is an ever-popular conversation piece throughout the island. It is also a safe subject matter to dwell on - unlike politics, or religion. Strangers from the north of the island who are holidaying in Kerry will freely discuss the weather situation with the natives. It is something that affects all of us, sometimes very deeply, when we depend on benign conditions to grow fruit, and other crops that are grown so effortlessly in other parts of Europe.

The same Lord who said "I do set my bow in the cloud, and it shall be for a token of a covenant between me and the earth." (Genesis 9v13), is He who is sovereign over earthquakes throughout the world, tornadoes in the Americas, melting glaciers in the Alps ... and wintry days in an Irish summer. He has lessons to teach the human race - both collectively and individually. I have no right to feel angry about a "grey day" for "he maketh his sun to rise on the evil and on the good, and sendeth rain on the just and the unjust." (Matthew 5v45) So many are suffering in our world today, which is something I know nothing about! Certainly we can, (and must) pray about weather conditions when lives are in danger, or when the livelihood of farmers is being affected. Let us never forget ... "Elias was a man subject to like passions as we are, and he prayed earnestly that it might not rain: and it rained not on the earth by the space of three years and six months. And he prayed again, and the heaven gave rain, and the earth brought forth her fruit." (James 5v17&18). With all the great advances in technology in recent years, people have found no way to drag clouds away from a blue sky, or create rain in the parched lands of the earth ... but "the effectual fervent prayer of a righteous man availeth much" (James 5v16). This is as true today, as it was in the days of Elijah!

Just a week after that wintry weekend I was to be found sitting outdoors, enjoying the warmth of that elusive Irish sunshine. I remembered the words of Paul: "...for I have learned, in whatsoever state I am, therewith to be content." (Phil. 4v11). I knew that I must, in a wider practical sense, apply these words to my own life. I read media reports on global warming, and yet God's word tells me: "While the earth remaineth, seedtime and harvest, and cold and heat, and summer and winter, and day and night shall not cease." (Gen. 8v22). And yet someday the earth will be subject to the ultimate trauma, for we read ... "But the day of the Lord will come as a thief in the night; in the which the heavens shall pass away with a great noise, and the elements shall melt with fervent heat, the earth also and the works that are therein shall be burned up." (2Pet. 3v10). Are you ready for this day? Remember that while we live in this, the 'day of grace,' His invitation stands in rain, hail, sun or snowstorm! To the Christian He says: "Seeing then that all these things shall be dissolved, what manner of persons ought ye to be in all holy conversation and godliness." (2Pet.3v11) "Nevertheless, we, according to his promise, look for new heavens and a new earth, wherein dwelleth righteousness." (2Pet. 3v13). With these crucial exhortations and wonderful promises, let us in the words of Peter ... "grow in grace, and in the knowledge of our Lord and Saviour Jesus Christ. To him be glory both now and for ever. Amen." (2Pet.3v18).

Lord, help me I pray to be content,
With rain or sun from heaven sent.
Instruct me Lord, that I might know,
The blessings that thou dost bestow.

A double rainbow near Stamullen, in Co. Meath – note the old tower
in the background.

(13)

"And Behold I Am with Thee, And Will Keep Thee
In All Places Whither Thou Goest…"
(Genesis 28v15)

(July 1st-July 15th)

My mouth was dry, and my heart racing, as the aircraft accelerated along the runway and rose shakily above the emerald 'patchwork quilt.' In recent years I had developed a phobia of flying, but today I had another reason to be afraid. "Well, here goes…" I turned to my daughter, who returned my nervous smile with a broad grin. Squeezing my hand she reassured me. "It'll be ok. Mum. Don't worry about a thing. This is probably the *safest* time to go!" I closed my eyes in prayer for our safety in the journey ahead and for our loved ones back home. How on earth had I got myself into this situation? Here we were, sitting above the little fluffy white clouds, bound for a destination that only two days ago had come under intensive terrorist attacks. And there was no going back!

It all started when my fifteen- year-old (like many fifteen-year-olds) informed us that she didn't want to go on the family holiday that year. "I would love to go to London for a few days instead," she announced… "But only with you, Mum." (Probably because she knew that she could 'wrap me around her little finger.') "Then I'll stay with Gran. and Granda, until you lot get back from hols."
"Oh really? Well, we'll see about that!" However, she *had* worked hard for her Junior Certificate Examinations, and eventually I conceded… "Would four nights in London be enough?" I asked. "You know (or maybe you don't) how expensive London can be!"
"Yep! That'll be fine. Thanks Mum."
Originally we had planned to fly out on Monday 4th July, returning on Friday 8th July. Then there was a change of plans, because of my husband's work schedule and the fact that he had to leave us to the airport. An economy flight was booked for Saturday 9th - to return on Wednesday 13th. The morning of 7th July, 2005 dawned, and as thousands of commuters were making their way onto

84

the London underground system, I was driving to our local supermarket in order to stock up on supplies for my husband, our other two daughters, and two cousins who were coming to stay in our absence. It was then that I first heard the devastating news. My eldest daughter sounded tearful on the mobile. "Mum, there have been terrible explosions in some London tube stations. I don't think you two will be going *anywhere* on Saturday…"

My fifteen-year-old was livid - but determined. "I've been looking forward to this trip for weeks. Why should we let this put us off?"

"But it's very serious - the tube system is down," I protested. "And can't you see the danger? The people behind this could well do it again! I think that we are crazy to go under the circumstances."

"I'm afraid they won't refund the cost of your flights," my husband told us, "although the manager of your accommodation has kindly offered not to charge, should you decide against going." For the next twenty-four hours I was suffering from insomnia, as I listened to news reports coming in of a rising death toll. Should we fly into such a situation? Then, alone in my bedroom, just hours before our proposed journey, I felt a wave of peace pass over me, as I read: "…And, behold, I am with thee, and will keep thee in all places whither thou goest, and will bring thee again into this land; for I will not leave thee, until I have done that which I have spoken of." (Gen. 29v15). "We'll go," I said, "and the Lord will protect us. It is in His hands. If He doesn't want us to go - this flight will be cancelled."

Although I also wandered about the wisdom of letting my teenager dictate the terms, I was trusting the Lord as we embarked upon this journey - yet I was still somewhat nervous! It had been many years since I last visited London and even then it had only been a temporary lodging place on a journey to somewhere else. Today that great city is heavily populated by many nationalities, including descendants of the 'Emerald Isle.' I was relieved that, at least, Irish nationals did not appear to be responsible for this evil.

Many of us could name them all - those organisations of terror (many of which have links with each other) which have destroyed life and property in countries throughout the world. Ireland, Britain, and Spain are numbered amongst those who have suffered at their hands. 'Suicide bombing,' however, is a relatively new phenomenon

– one which has greatly affected Israel, Iraq and U.S.A. in recent years. The word 'Kamikaze' was first used in 13th century Japan to describe a storm (or 'divine wind') which protected the Japanese from advancing Mongols, Koreans and Chinese, but the word took on a whole new meaning during World War 2, when it was used to describe pilots who launched 'suicide attacks' on their enemies. Nevertheless, perhaps it was patriotism and hunger for power in the region which fired their efforts, not 'religious' fervour. How strangely contradictory are the terms 'holy war,' and 'blessed war!'

Saturday dawned, and our flight was not cancelled, but quite late because of heightened security. Due to the actions of a certain potential 'shoe bomber,' we were now suffering the inconvenience of having to remove our shoes for airport security. Placing these and other requested objects on the tray, I hoped for their safe arrival through the detector, and stood waiting expectantly at the other end. It is true that even the most harmless looking object can be used for deadly ends! Here, I could not help but think of a spiritual parallel. As Christians, all we are, and all we have, is His. "What? Know ye not that your body is the temple of the Holy Ghost which is in you, which ye have of God, and ye are not your own? For ye are bought with a price: therefore glorify God in your body, and in your spirit, which are God's." (1Cor. 6v19&20). We must be prepared to put all on His altar: possessions, interests, talents, friendships and work… Indeed He has the power to remove anything from us in an instant. If anything which I had placed on that conveyor belt for detection had proved to be potentially dangerous to myself and those around me, it would have been instantly taken away - and justifiably so. We are "the clay:" He "the Potter" (Romans 9v21). We are "the branches:" He is "the vine." (John 15v5). He has much pruning and shaping to do when a soul comes to Him by faith, but what wonderful things God can do with willing souls *in an instant*! Undoubtedly, it is very often lack of faith on our part which delays the blessing that He wants to give us.

Strangely my fear of flying had lost its intensity as we climbed into the 'great bird' that would take us through the clouds, for I was now trusting that the Saviour would protect in this also. I have heard of one sportsman who refuses to fly anywhere; he prefers to make long journeys by sea and rail, rather than be subject to the "law of aero-dynamics!" However, I listened with interest to a speaker at a Christian conference, who was also apprehensive about flying. Comfortingly he had concentrated on the spiritual side of flying. "Granted," he told us, "planes may crash - but cars much more often. But you know when we are way up there, we are no longer under the law of gravity - we are under a *different* law." Surely too, as Christians, we are under *a different law*. Flying through the clouds, I experience the 'law of aero-dynamics' and when I walk with Jesus each day, I am no longer under the law of "sin and death" but I live by faith on the wings of His grace. "Knowing this, that our old man is crucified with him, that the body of sin might be destroyed, that henceforth *we should not serve sin*. For he that is dead is freed from sin." (Rom. 6v6&7). If He takes precedence in our lives, and we live by faith (in *His strength*) above the world and all its snares, ceasing to serve sin, then... "Sin shall not have dominion over you: for ye are not under the law, but under grace." (Rom 6v14).

Of course two laws or two masters cannot govern us at the one time. One must ultimately take control. "What then? Shall we sin, because we are not under the law, but under grace? God forbid. Know ye not, that to whom ye yield yourselves servants to obey; whether of sin unto death, or of obedience unto righteousness? But God be thanked, that ye were the servants of sin, but ye have obeyed from the heart that form of doctrine which was delivered you. Being then made free from sin, ye became the servants of righteousness." (Rom. 6v15-18). "There is therefore now no condemnation to them which are in Christ Jesus, *who walk not after the flesh, but after the spirit*. For the law of the Spirit of life in Christ Jesus hath made me free from the law of sin and death." (Rom. 8v1&2)

What comfort I found in His Word during the journey! Still apprehensive about what we may encounter in London, I prayed during the flight, and opened my Bible to find these words... "But I will deliver thee in that day, saith the Lord: and thou shalt not be given into the hand of the men of whom thou art afraid. For I will surely deliver thee, and thou shalt not fall by the sword, but thy life shall be for a prey unto thee: because thou hast put thy trust in me, saith the Lord." (Jer. 39v17&18). Just as these words comforted Jeremiah, shut up in a prison around 590 B.C., they now brought comfort to a woman sitting in an aircraft, some 2595 years later!

Again I read... "Trust in the Lord with all thine heart; and lean not unto thine own understanding. In all thy ways acknowledge him, and he shall direct thy paths." (Prov. 3v5&6).

Attempting to land at Gatwick, I was alarmed as the aircraft quickly ascended again, and seemed to be circling the airport for some time. "We cannot land," announced the pilot, "owing to the fact that another plane is on the runway." Surely, too, a soul cannot expect the Lord to come into his life, when there is a major obstruction to His entrance and presence in that life? The "Rich Young Ruler" wanted the Lord's entrance into his life, but he was not willing to 'clear the runway' - to put God before riches. (Luke 18v18-23). At the same time we should never forget that... "The things which are impossible with men are possible with God." (Luke 18v27)

Touching down on the cleared runway, we were confronted by the shimmering heat of a summer's day - and the tense atmosphere of a crowded airport. Armed police mingled here and there with the passengers. Gentlemen of Asian and Middle-Eastern origin sadly became targets for scrutinizing glances. I remembered when I too, became the target for such glances, despite my British passport. I was young, weary, and suffering from a combination of sunstroke and 'flu, as I stood in one of London's airports, having travelled overland across Europe. (It is so long ago, that I don't remember which airport it was!) Feeling ill, I pleaded weakly with the well-built security woman... "Careful... presents wrapped for home..." I faltered, wiping beads of sweat from my forehead. Frisking me roughly, and tearing the presents open, I can still remember her words, as she glared at me... "That's *your* story, isn't it?" I felt that, as far as she was concerned, people of my origin were all the same (whatever our background) although *both* of our countries had suffered at the hands of evil men in those days.

'All the same, yes, those Muslim ladies in their chadors *do* look all the same,' I thought, as I watched them walk down Oxford Street some days later. Surely none of these would rejoice in the death of a son (or daughter) for any cause...? But behind the all-embracing black, lay individual thoughts, aspirations, worries... Each veiled figure, a soul for whom my Lord had died... "Mum! Come on! What are you dreaming about? There's so much to see, and we haven't many days here... Hey, wasn't there a real buzz about Buckingham Palace yesterday? All those elderly people with their medals, celebrating sixty years since the end of World War II. It was great that you got a photo of the Queen!"

"I was just thinking," I said, my eyes suddenly blurred with tears, as I watched her stride ahead, confident, walking swiftly towards the inevitable. Womanhood lay ahead. I desperately didn't want to lose her in the crowds... I prayed silently, that within her freedom, she would make the right choices. Life was a minefield, and I feared for my children.

One night I tried to sleep through noises I was unaccustomed to. Instead of a lone fox barking in the darkness, a curlew at dusk, the 'dawn chorus,' or cattle and sheep in the fields, I was hearing ambulance and police sirens, traffic, and the rumble of the metro deep below us. Then I thought of all the inhabitants of that great city - everyone from those homeless junkies in the subway, and that white-faced girl (covered in bruises) who approached me for money - to the stock brokers, the Prime Minister and the members of the Royal family. Yes, every city has its 'dregs of society' and its 'dignitaries,' but to my Lord every soul is equally precious in His sight and He is "no respecter of persons." (Acts 10v34). Oh that all would humbly turn to Him by faith, and put their trust in the shed blood of the Lord Jesus Christ!

I remember reading many stories of personal tragedy in the newspapers at that time. A mother could not find her daughter, and somehow dreaded seeing that unfinished novel (that she knew she was writing) in her bedroom. A husband had lost a loving wife; children had lost fathers and mothers; a brother had lost a sister; a heartbroken friend had lost her young flatmate. How the Lord looks down with compassion on those wounded souls and bodies, and how He wants to heal those shattered lives and broken hearts! And how apt are the words of Isaiah 61v1-3: "The spirit of the Lord God is upon me; because the Lord hath anointed me to preach good tidings unto the meek; he hath set me to bind up the broken-hearted, to proclaim liberty to the captives, and the opening of the prison to them that are bound; To proclaim the acceptable year of the Lord, and the day of vengeance of our God; to comfort all that mourn; To appoint unto them that mourn in Zion, to give unto them beauty for ashes, the oil of joy for mourning, the garment of praise for the spirit of heaviness; that they might be called trees of righteousness, the planting of the Lord, that he might be glorified..."

Before embarking on this trip, I prayed that I might meet (and be encouraged) by even just one fellow Christian in that great city. One bright morning as I stood outside a large store waiting for my daughter, I saw my answer to prayer. Very small, very humble, a little black man walked the pavement, with a powerful voice - and an open Bible. Some people looked at him pityingly as he preached the message of salvation, in the wake of the London bombings, but what touched me most about him was that he was crying. Walking towards him, but not wanting to interrupt his message, I touched his shoulder and gave him some words of encouragement. "Praise God! A sister in the Lord!" He shouted, before continuing to preach his way down the street. After this I was encouraged, too, that those who saw the encounter had witnessed something very wonderful. "By this shall all men know that ye are my disciples, if ye have love one to another." (John 13v35).

Life *is* a minefield as people travel to and fro upon the face of our globe and the spectre of international terrorism increasingly casts its ugly shadow upon us. But God is sovereign! Let those of us who name His precious name, and have occasion to travel, make our journeys prayerfully and with wisdom as the years lie ahead - witnessing always for the Master *wherever* we go. Who knows what effect one single tract, or word in season, may have upon the soul who receives it?

"I've just made a fifteen hour flight from Mexico, on the plane before this one," said the lady who sat beside me on our return journey. "We were at a wedding over there! I'll just be so relieved to be safely back in Ireland," she added.

"So will I - although I didn't go as far as you," I replied with a smile, as our plane dropped in altitude close to the airport. "Can I give you something to read? I've put my trust in Someone who tells me that He is with me in all places wherever I go."

"Oh thanks. I promise I'll read it later when I locate my specs - wherever they are. I'm so disorganised when I'm travelling!"

Soon our voices grew eerily muffled, with the increased noise of the aircraft as it came in to land. Once more closing my eyes in silent prayer, I thanked my Lord for bringing us safely home, as our plane softly thudded down on my beloved 'emerald quilt.' But surely the only safe place on earth is to be firmly within His will, for is *anywhere* safe, when we are outside His loving arms? But so long as we "take refuge in the shadow of His wings," (Psalm 57v1), then the joyful words of Psalm 91 will be our portion forevermore… "He that dwelleth in the secret place of the most High shall abide under the shadow of the Almighty. I will say of the Lord, He is my refuge and my fortress: my God; in him will I trust. Surely he shall deliver thee from the snare of the fowler, and from the noisome pestilence. He shall cover thee with his feathers, and under his wings shalt thou trust: his truth shall be thy shield and buckler. Thou shalt not be afraid for the terror by night; nor for the arrow that flieth by day; Nor for the pestilence that walketh in darkness; nor for the destruction that wasteth at noonday. A thousand shall fall at thy side, and ten thousand at thy right hand; but it shall not come nigh thee." (Psalm 91v1-7)

In days of old His children fled,
Through the Red Sea's dried-up bed.
The Guide who lit all Israel's way,
By fire at night, and cloud by day,
Ever lives for all who journey Home,
Where streets of gold, not earthly dust,
Their lovely feet shall roam.

A couple with their horse-drawn caravan in Co. Wicklow

"There's a Flag Flown High – From the Castle of my Heart!"
(Romans 12v18)

(July 16th- July 31st)

We had driven for miles that glorious July day, along one of Northern Ireland's scenic coastlines. The blue sea shimmered in sunlight, as we admired the rugged beauty of the landscape across the peninsula. Evening found us in a lovely little harbour town, but by now much traffic had slowed our progress. "Why is everything moving so slowly?" I whispered, as I wound down my window in the stuffy car. Just then I could hear the distant sound of drums and accordions playing some familiar melody. "A band!" one of the children shouted. "That's why we're stuck in traffic. Hope we see it soon!" But before the band came into view, we saw first the fascinating array of banners and colourful flags flown high and to the forefront, blowing in the sea breeze.

Suddenly I noticed something else too - the hostile crowd that had gathered across the street. Someone shouted at those who paraded. I hoped and prayed that there would be no further hostilities that evening, and thankfully I believe that the proceedings concluded peacefully - but I can still remember those flags flapping in the summer evening breeze, and the variety of expressions on the faces of those who observed…

Some years later we found ourselves again in traffic, this time travelling south of the border. Gaelic football supporters were driving swiftly towards the latter, their little flags and colourful ensigns rippling triumphantly in the breeze. This time the atmosphere was jubilant and light-hearted. At the sight of those colourful emblems of victory, even opponents of the team in question would cheer good-humouredly and wave. This, however, is not always so under similar circumstances. We are all acquainted with media reports of football hooliganism, and certain colourful emblems which inspire fury in the hearts of opponents. "It's like showing a red rag to a bull" is a familiar old saying. Indeed (I am ashamed to say) I can recall watching a bullfight in Barcelona many years ago. I felt sorry for that bull as it charged in fury towards inevitable doom...

Somehow all of these thoughts came together as I studied with interest a little book I had discovered, on the history of all the flags of the nations of the world. There were flags which were used to distinguish between friend and foe on the battlefield; flags on sea-faring vessels; flags for signalling; flags for sport and recreation and flags for religious celebration. What fascinated me, though, were the complete array of flags currently in use by each nation, and the fact that each design and symbol was of historical and political significance. Many emblems (such as the hated swastika in Germany) are no longer in use on flags - but can be seen on graffitied walls, and continue to instil fear in the hearts of those who remember truly terrible days. Little nations, such as Lithuania, reverted to use of their old flags after gaining independence. On the Lithuanian flag, for example, yellow represents wheat and freedom from want; green symbolises its forests and renewed hope; while red symbolises patriotism and courage. It is interesting to note how many nations have been born out of warfare and shed blood, represented by the red on their flags, while the Islamic country of Saudi Arabia carries the Muslim statement of faith and a sword! On the other hand, the flag of the Republic of Ireland signifies peace between 'orange and green', while the flag of Cyprus, with its two olive branches, portrays peace and prosperity between the Greek and Turkish communities. However, since the Turkish invasion in 1974, the two parts of the island also fly the national flags of Greece and Turkey.

As the Lord looks down upon the earth He sees democracies, dictatorships, divisions, injustices, famine, war, evil laws, rampant terrorism, human trafficking and hostage taking. But beyond the flags of nations, with their colours, races and creeds, He sees, knows and loves each individual within those nations. Indeed, as we can see from His Word, there is *no one* for whom His precious blood has not been shed. (1John 2v2; 1Tim. 2v6; 1Tim 4v10; 1John 4v14). It is His will that *all* should come to repentance (2Pet. 3v9; 1Tim 2v4), and share eternity with Him in heaven. Of the Christian, the Bible tells us ... "There is neither Jew nor Greek, there is neither bond nor free, there is neither male nor female: for ye are all one in Christ

Jesus. And if ye be Christ's, then are ye Abraham's seed, and heirs according to the promise." (Gal. 3v28&29) Whether we are black, white, yellow, coffee-coloured or of 'Planter or Gael' background makes no difference when we are true and loyal subjects of *His* Kingdom. The Christian cannot be 'neatly filed away' in precise little compartments governing colour, race, creed, gender or class. Out of every nation they are those who, by faith, have been born again of the Spirit of God. A 'peculiar people' (Titus 2v14) they put God first in their lives; the Bible is their guidebook through life's journey; and they love their Saviour, even unto death. The verse: "If it be possible, as much as lieth within you, live peaceably with all men," (Rom. 12v18) is applied, in practical terms to their daily lives. Also, as citizens of the 'heavenly kingdom' on a temporary journey through life's short day, their mission is to reach others with the love of the Saviour, but not to be "conformed to this world" (Rom. 12v2). According to His promise they look for that day which is described in Isaiah 65v17... "For, behold, I create new heavens and a new earth: and the former shall not be remembered, nor come into mind."

In Rev.7v9&10 we read: "After this I beheld, and, lo, a great multitude, which no man could number, of all nations, and kindreds, and people, and tongues, stood before the throne, and before the Lamb, clothed with white robes, and palms in their hands; And cried with a loud voice saying, "Salvation to our God which sitteth upon the throne, and unto the Lamb." Are you ready for that glorious Day, and will you stand with the ransomed of the nations singing (not national anthems) but praises to the Lamb, and waving (not your nation's flag) but palms of peace? Surely "Jehova-nissi" (the Lord is my banner) is a powerful word to those who serve the "king?" As a child I remember being taught a little chorus:

> *"There's a flag flown high*
> *From the castle of my heart*
> *And the King is in residence there."*

I sang the words but did not have 'the heart experience' until I was twenty-five years old. Now, thank God, I have been set free to sing those words 'in spirit and in truth.' Remember, He loves you, and it is His will that you repent and ask Him into your heart now, for He has paid the ultimate price for you as an individual - whatever your skin colour, your nation's flag, or your team's colours! And it is His will that some wonderful day you will be allied with those who sing a new song...

"Thou art worthy to take the book,
and to open the seals thereof:
for thou wast slain,
and hast redeemed us to God by the blood
out of every kindred, and tongue, and people, and nation;
and hast made us unto our God kings and priests;
and we shall reign on the earth."
(Rev.5v9&10

Down through the annals of history we may read of how invading armies arrived suddenly and unexpectedly to conquer. Some day Jesus, too, will return very suddenly to conquer and to claim His own. Just as the white flag indicates surrender and peace to an invading army, our white robes will show our total surrender to He who loved us and gave Himself for us. That dazzling white may not always guarantee safety where the armies of the world are concerned, but it will where *He* is concerned! Furthermore, unlike an invading army, he wants the very best for us and He wants to share His riches with us for all eternity.

In Revelations 6v17, we read: "For the great day of his wrath is come; and who shall be able to stand?" Surely *only* those out of every nation, and under every flag, who have "washed their robes, and made them white in the blood of the Lamb." (Rev. 7v14). Oh that all who read would be numbered amongst that "great multitude, which no man could number!"

Flags that fly o'er east and west,
Flags with colouring or crest,
Banners thrust far high above -
But "His banner over me was love!"
(Song of Solomon 2v4)

Re-enactment at Battle of Boyne (1690) site, near Drogheda.

(15)

Words of Gold - On a Vessel of Old
(Phil. 3v7&8)

(August 1st - August 15th)

I remember a certain tranquil mid-summer afternoon, when the sun beat down upon ripening cornfields and little fluffy white clouds drifted in heavenly blue skies. Only birds on the wing, softly sweeping across the far horizon, disturbed the motionless scene. Being young and energetic (then!) I took out my old bicycle and went cycling down leafy country lanes, in what is known as Ireland's 'orchard county' - Armagh. In those days my summers, for the most part, were carefree and I remember with affection those familiar haunts of youthful days.

On that particular day I cycled past the entrance to Castledillon Domain. Here, an imposing old mansion stood on a hill (as it does to this day) its fading grandeur reflected in the peaceful waters of a lake, where swans and water hens made their abode. Built for Sir George Molyneux, and finished in 1845, it had seen a variety of occupants since then, including psychiatric patients, and more recently the British Army, during Northern Ireland's troubles. Sir Capel Molyneaux, who once lived there, was said to have declared on his death-bed… "Oh fair Castledillon, how can I leave thee?" As with all of mankind, he was "going the way of all the earth." (Josh. 23v14; 1Kings 2v2) but he could not bear to leave the beauty of his earthly estate.

Cycling onwards, the level road at that point was no trouble at all. But then my journey took me over some undulating countryside. Thinking about it now many years later, I can see that it is just like the Christian life itself! The hills were a stress, but they brought their rewards, in the form of beautiful views. Spiritually speaking, when we have a tough up-hill struggle we can see clearly when we emerge triumphantly from that crisis. There on that peaceful mountain top the air is clear and we are closer to the Saviour than ever before. Temptation overcome certainly leaves us spiritually stronger too.

Looking around from one of the hills in this area, I can see in one direction, the peaks of the Sperrin Mountains and in the other, the spires of the Cathedral City of Armagh. When I see a magnificent view I am sometimes reminded of the temptation of Jesus, which is recorded in Luke, Chapter 4. Jesus, "being full of the Holy Ghost returned from Jordan, and was led by the Spirit into the wilderness." (Verse 1) We read how He fasted for forty days, and during that time was constantly tempted of the devil. It is interesting to note that, with every iniquitous temptation thrown at Him, Jesus in turn quoted scripture - which the devil knows, but hates! For example, when the devil asked Jesus to command a stone to be turned into bread, His reply was: *"It is written*, That man shall not live by bread alone, but by every word of God," (verse 4). What better way to counteract the 'evil one,' than with scripture!

At one point, the devil taking Jesus up into "an high mountain, shewed unto him all the kingdoms of the world in a moment of time," (verse 5). His words to Jesus were: "All this power will I give thee, and the glory of them: for that is delivered unto me; and to whomsoever I will give it. If thou therefore wilt worship me, all shall be thine." (Verses 6&7).

Jesus replied: "Get thee behind me, Satan: *for it is written*, Thou shalt worship the Lord thy God, and him only shalt thou serve." (Verse 8). How often the devil uses riches, land and the things of this world, as bait for the children of men. Surely, if our possessions consist of nothing but the tangible, we are most miserable and without eternal hope?

After some time I came to a lovely rural area where I stopped close to an old deserted period residence and laid my bicycle down. As I strolled through the lush green grass, I noticed what looked like an old piece of china, half-buried in the undergrowth. Loosening the grip of the grass around it, I pulled it up, and examined it with curiosity. What I had discovered was an unusual old pot, which once had handles on each side. Cracked in many places, but beautifully designed, it bore a bouquet of flowers on one side, and on the other side was printed the following, in fine gold italics...

"The loss of gold is great
The loss of time is more
But the loss of Christ is such a loss
That no man can restore."

As a Christian, very young in the faith at that time, these words made a very strong impression on me. I remember standing there, alone in that meadow, tracing those lovely words with my finger, and then I prayed that all loved ones and acquaintances might see this truth for themselves! Today, nearly three decades later, I still treasure the old pot, and reflect upon its words. The years have taken their toll on its glazed surface, but the golden words remain perfect and unchanging. In a sense it reminds me of a well-worn old Bible. The book itself may one day perish, but "the word of our God shall stand for ever." (Isaiah 40v8).

Indeed those golden words are as true today, as they were when they were painted on (perhaps over a century ago) and in that sense they *do* remind me of God's Word. "Heaven and earth shall pass away; but my words shall not pass away," Jesus tells us in Mark 13v31. Unlike God's Word, the written words of mankind (despite their wisdom) may pass away, and be lost to future generations - but the truth that they represent in the Bible endures forever.

Firstly, I think of the gold - a highly esteemed most precious metal from time immemorial, and yet ... "The law of thy mouth is better unto me than thousands of gold and silver." (Psalm 119v72). In 2Chron. 9v20 we learn that "All the drinking vessels of King Solomon were of gold, and all the vessels of the house of the forest of Lebanon were of pure gold: none were of silver; it was not anything accounted of in the days of Solomon." Although "King Solomon passed all the kings of the earth in riches and wisdom," Jesus asks us a very profound question in Mark 8v36: "For what shall it profit a man, if he shall gain the whole world, and lose his own soul?" Furthermore, Psalm 49v16&17 advises us: "Be not thou afraid when one is made rich, when the glory of his house is increased; For when he dieth he shall carry nothing away: his glory shall not descend after him." The words of Psalm 49v6&7 also confirm to us that *riches cannot either buy ourselves, or our deceased loved ones a home in heaven…* "They that trust in their wealth, and boast themselves in the multitude of their riches; None of them can by any means redeem his brother, nor give to God a ransom for him: (For the redemption of their soul is precious, and it ceaseth forever :)" The gold, in a sense, represents anything material that is precious to us on this earth; and so all of these things must be sacrificed to His blood, in the face of Christ's great sacrifice for us at Calvary. This is beautifully portrayed in Isaac Watt's lovely hymn: "When I Survey the Wondrous Cross", from which I quote the final verse:

"Were the whole realm of nature mine,
That were an offering far too small;
Love so amazing, so divine,
Demands my soul, my life, my all."

Then I think of that very valuable (though intangible) commodity - 'time'. "Time and tide wait for no man" is an old and very true proverb. I love the tick of my grandmother's old clock upon the window-sill, but it is a 'timely' reminder that every minute is precious and should not be wasted. I think of the twenty-five years of my life before I became a Christian. Most of these years could be summed up in the apt words of the first verse of Wm. R. Newell's hymn "At Calvary"…

"Years I spent in vanity and pride
Caring not my Lord was crucified,
Knowing not it was for me He died
On Calvary."

What a waste this time was, and yet the sins of those wasted years have been drowned forever in the great sea of the Lord's loving forgiveness! (Micah 7v19). Time is such an important element today, and so we have microwaves, 'fast food' outlets, jet planes, fast cars and fast communication networks. The wise people of bygone eras would have been horrified by the latter, and yet they too regarded the loss of time as more disastrous than the loss of gold, for gold may be recovered by some means, but this is not so with time.

101

However, we are reminded of a strange fact in Rev. 10v6 ... "that there should be time no longer." It is difficult for us to conceive of a situation where some day, even time, with all its pull on our lives, shall be vanquished forever. If we belong to the Lord, we shall rest forever in the light of His presence and glory, no longer troubled by the pressures of life on earth. The first verse of that well-known hymn by J.M. Black surely brings joyful encouragement to the Christian - but a disturbing question to those who are outside of Christ...

"When the trumpet of the Lord shall sound,
and time shall be no more,
And the morning breaks, eternal, bright and fair;
When the saved of earth shall gather
over on the other shore,
And the roll is called up yonder,
I'll be there."

In the light of eternity, gold is nothing and "time shall be no more." Are you ready for that day when the trumpet shall sound, and time shall be extinguished forever? Is your name written in the Lamb's Book of Life? In Rev. 21v27 we read of the New Jerusalem... "And there shall in no wise enter into it any thing that defileth, neither whatsoever worketh abomination, or maketh a lie: but they which are written in the Lamb's book of life." Remember ... "the loss of Christ is such a loss, that no man can restore," and "Neither their silver nor their gold shall be able to deliver them in the day of the Lord's wrath..." (Zeph. 1v18), but... "Whosoever shall call upon the name of the Lord shall be saved." (Rom. 10v13). Oh that the following words of Paul would apply to all who read... "For God, who commanded the light to shine out of darkness, hath shined in our hearts, to give the light of the knowledge of the glory of God in the face of Jesus Christ. But we have this treasure in earthen vessels, that the excellency of the power may be of God, and not of us." (2Cor. 4v6&7).

I found some treasure long ago-
A treasure only His can know.
For nothing matters - time, nor gold,
But that His face I would behold!

Castledillon today, lying derelict at the time of writing.

(16)

"Cast thy bread upon the waters:
For thou shalt find it after many days..."
(Eccl. 11v1)

(August 16th - August 31st)

Many years ago when I was without Christ, I travelled with a friend from Northern Ireland by land and sea for a holiday in Belgium. One day we visited a vast cathedral, which was situated across the border in France. Entering that magnificent building, we hesitated for a moment in the outer porch, where people generally sign a visitors' book or make donations. There, amongst the rest of the musty literature containing information about the cathedral was a small leaflet with some Bible verses on it. I often wonder who had left it there, but God's Word in this humble pamphlet spoke to me. Subsequently there followed a disturbing number of days when His "still small voice" spoke to me so strongly, that I could no longer bear it. It was upon my return home, on the beautiful evening of Monday 28th August, 1978, after a fierce spiritual battle, that I crossed from darkness into light, when I asked Jesus to be my Saviour.

It must be said that the great cathedral itself, and its atmosphere of imposing quietness, brought no solace to my feelings of conviction. In Acts 17v24-29 Paul told those superstitious Athenians: "God that made the world and all things therein, seeing that he is Lord of heaven and earth, dwelleth not in temples made with hands; Neither is worshipped with men's hands, as though he needed any thing, seeing he giveth to all life, and breath, and all things; And hath made of one blood all nations of men for to dwell on all the face of the earth, and hath determined the times before appointed, and the bounds of their habitation; That they should seek the Lord, if haply they might find him, though he be not far from every one of us: For in him we live, and move, and have our being; as certain also of your poets have said, For we are also his offspring. Forasmuch then as we are the offspring of God, we ought not to think that the Godhead is like unto gold, or silver, or stone, graven by art and man's device."

Often as Christians we may have occasion to visit such great cathedrals, and other places of historical interest, being fully aware that "the most High dwelleth not in temples made with hands..." (Acts 7v48). These same sentiments were uttered by Solomon, after the building of his temple... "But will God indeed dwell on the earth? Behold, the heaven and heaven of heavens cannot contain thee; how much less this house that I have builded?" (1Kings 8v27). Nevertheless, our visits to such places can present marvellous opportunities to speak a word in season, or to leave the pure Word of God in some appropriate place, as a witness to others. Before finding the verses in that cathedral, I had already been under conviction - so much so that I had brought my Bible on that journey. I had asked for it as a gift the previous Christmas, saying that I wanted to read it for its 'literary value.' How delighted my parents, as Christians, must have been when I asked for that gift!

As well as the Bible in its conventional form, I am also convinced that the Lord uses His Word in the form of tracts, posters and other literature distributed by Christians. Sometimes they are to be found in unconventional places, and are an excellent way to reach people who would not normally read the Bible. Often, as a young non-Christian, I would have been offered tracts on the streets of towns and cities, and I always politely accepted them, although I had confined all things spiritual to the back of my mind, and to the recesses of many pockets! Nonetheless, each tract given to me made a very significant contribution to my growing feelings of uneasiness. I remember being given a tract by a Salvation Army member while socialising in a very un-Christian like environment. How ashamed it had made me feel!

One evening not long after my conversion, I heard the Lord speak strongly to me once again, but this time He was asking me to do something for Him, and in a sense it seemed like a strange request. It was a dark, cold and damp windy night as I sat in my little bedroom, hearing that 'still small voice' urging me to get dressed again and go with a tract down the lonely avenue and across the busy road to the public telephone kiosk. I was weary after a full day's work, but to this day that small incident stands out in my mind and I am so glad that I was obedient, for I feel certain that it was intended for some specific person. Was it that lorry driver who drew up in the darkness of the night…?

I can recall also, the old 'sandwich boards' which were worn at various events, and sometimes while distributing tracts on the streets. On each side there would be printed the powerful Word of God - something rarely seen in public nowadays.   Texts printed on hoardings, bus-stop shelters and other prominent places are a silent but stunning tribute to God's Word and its power to arrest the soul and convict of sin.   To the Christian they can be a wonderful encouragement and a cheering reminder that 'this world is not our home.' Even to see the precious name of 'Jesus' written on a text in a public place, somehow touches the hearts of those who know the Saviour, like no other name can.   John Newton, once an infidel, but marvellously saved to write many hymns, including the famous "Amazing Grace," also wrote the following beautiful hymn, from which I quote the first verse…

> *"How sweet the Name of Jesus sounds*
> *In a believer's ear!*
> *It soothes his sorrows, heals his wounds,*
> *And drives away his fear."*

On the other hand for those who are unsaved, Biblical texts can be a vital source of that conviction that is necessary before salvation. It is no wonder that we read in Hebrews 4v12: "For the word of God is quick, and powerful, and sharper than any two-edged sword, piercing even to the dividing asunder of soul and spirit, and of the joints and marrow, and is a discerner of the thoughts and intents of the heart."

Sadly, there are nations in today's world where God's Word, in any form, is prohibited.   I read of someone who once visited Albania during its Communist heyday, and witnessed the following coldly official words on a railway hoarding… "There is no God." Surely… *"The fool hath said in his heart*, There is no God!" (Psalm 14v1). After years of political turmoil, Albania today is one of the poorest countries in Europe, but despite its severe restrictions on Christians over the years, they have survived!   Who knows how long it will be before our own nation may adopt this stance? Those in positions of power have become so concerned with 'political correctness,' that they have lost sight of the truth. Not so long ago I had the idea of inserting Bible verses in a 'free-ads' paper, having previously noted that others were permitted to put in their 'thanks to saints for prayers answered.' At first those I dealt with willingly included my specified verses each week. Then, after just a short time the opposition came. "I have been instructed not to take these verses any more," said the voice on the telephone. When asked why, he replied: "What you are stating could bring offence - it's like a political statement. I'm sorry, I'm just taking orders." Opposition also came in the form of a text message to my mobile phone. (I had felt that I should include this with the verses, as I may have been able to help someone). "Stop preaching at us!" read one response. I read the words with amusement, but sadness. There is no doubt that the Word of God often brings great offence - something which Christians should not try to dilute, because they are afraid of hurting unsaved acquaintances. If people are to be saved, they firstly need to recognise the basic fact that they are lost. Ultimately it is what they 'do with Jesus,' that will determine eternity for them. "As it is written, Behold I lay in si-on a stumblingstone and rock of offence: and whosoever believeth on him shall not be ashamed." (Rom. 9v33).

Has the Lord put a burden in your heart today, to do something new (or old!) to win souls for Him? Remember the words of Daniel 11v32... "the people that do know their God shall be strong and do exploits." The evil one will try, by any means, to dissuade us, but ... "The Lord is my light and my salvation; whom shall I fear? The Lord is the strength of my life; of whom shall I be afraid?" (Psalm 27v1). Whether we are at home or abroad, it is a good idea to carry some Christian literature with us, that we may spread the gospel; although we should be fully convinced in our own minds about the content of that which we propose to distribute! Pray much about the literature itself, and for those who will receive it, that God will prepare their hearts, for "the preparations of the heart in man, and the answer of the tongue, is from the Lord." (Proverbs 16v1)

Therefore, as Christians, let us (in the words of Jesus), "work the works of him that sent me, while it is day: the night cometh, when no man can work." (John 9v4). Remember that "He that observeth the wind shall not sow; and he that regardeth the clouds shall not reap." (Eccl. 11v4) If, however, you have never trusted Jesus as your Saviour, remember that some day God's words will judge us all, to the extent that our eternal destiny will depend on how we have responded to it. "He that is not with me is against me: and he that gathereth not with me scattereth." (Luke 11v23). "For whosoever shall be ashamed of me and my words, of him shall the Son of man be ashamed, when he shall come in his own glory, and in his Father's, and of the holy angels." (Luke 9v26).

Come raise His banner to the sky,
And let His words be seen on high -
Come spread the word to sinful men
That Jesus died and rose again!

Text on the farm of Jack Hutchinson, near Armagh.

108

(17)

Indian Summer Heartaches - And a Light through the Mist
(Proverbs 4v18)

(September 1st- September 15th)

"Where has she gone?" I sighed, as I ran through the long dewy grass calling her name, that early autumn morning. She was due to go in for a morning's orientation at her new Secondary School that very day, but I had found the back door open and my daughter was missing. I called her name as I walked, but all I could hear was the cheerful chirping of small birds as they fluttered amongst the brambles, and the crone of pigeons in nearby trees. For the first time I noticed the beauty of that dawning autumn, somehow incongruous in the light of present problems. Yes, it was going to be a beautiful day, but wasn't all of nature supposed to be in mourning when the children had to return to school?

A pale sun, barely visible through the mist, was rising in the sky and dew gleamed on the briars that scratched my legs as I walked. The season of fading leaves, laden apple trees, blackberry bushes - and back-to-school adventures had begun. For some individuals that meant a challenge, excitement and new friends, but for others it was nothing short of a nightmare. I remembered another autumn morning like this one. Having left the children to Primary School, I was driving past a large local day/boarding school, when I noticed a boy standing alone outside its great walls. Somehow I have never forgotten the terrified expression on his young face. It bore the look of someone who was deeply unhappy, and wanted desperately to escape. Now years later, I had seen the same look on my daughter's face earlier this September morning. I urgently wanted to find her, reassure her and bring her home, and I prayed, as I walked, that the Lord would bring me to her. 'Surely,' I thought, 'home is where the most important issues in all of life should be learned?'

To a great extent, the role and influence of parents in their children's lives has changed radically over the last century. With an increasing number of *both* parents employed in the workforce, we have 'the door-key children.' Television and the Internet have become 'universal babysitters,' and teachers are left to deal with problems that should really have been resolved in the home. Most 'politically correct' individuals today would find the words of 1Tim. 5v14, difficult to accept... "I will therefore that the younger women marry, bear children, guide the house, give none occasion to the adversary to speak reproachfully." Fathers, too, are exhorted to "provoke not your children to wrath: but bring them up in the nurture and admonition of the Lord." (Eph. 6v4). Without a doubt, the timeless Word of God asks for our obedience today, as much as it did in centuries gone by.

All through that long summer I had noticed, with interest, the teenagers in our locality. Many of them looked bored, restless, aimlessly texting on their mobile 'phones or kicking a tin can around. However, some were more actively causing trouble wherever they could. Certainly, 'the devil finds work for idle hands to do!' My older teenagers had gone for 'a pleasant walk in the countryside' on one of the long summer evenings, when they were almost run over by a 'joy-rider' only a mile from our home. Aiming his (probably stolen) car at them, he threateningly drove at them, thinking that they had telephoned the Gardai because they had seen his reckless driving. On their return home, they were still very shaken and *I* telephoned the Gardai. What a tremendous responsibility parents have for their children! Unfortunately schools, too, are no longer 'safe havens,' since many are infiltrated by drug-pushers. The words of Eccles.11v9&10 are clearly intended for the young: "Rejoice, O young man, in thy youth; and let thy heart cheer thee in the days of thy youth, and walk in the ways of thine heart, and in the sight of thine eyes: but know thou, that for all these things God will bring thee into judgement. Therefore remove sorrow from thy heart, and put away evil from thy flesh: for childhood and youth are vanity."

Now, as I searched for my little girl, I felt to blame for this present situation. Where had I gone wrong, and why did she have such an aversion to something that most children take in their stride? Just then as I frantically called her name, I heard her nearby. Through the early morning mist a shaft of sunlight shone warmly on both of us, as I hugged her with relief, and gently encouraged her to come home. During breakfast I did not mention the taboo subject which had caused so much friction, as I could see that she needed to eat properly. 'No,' I thought. 'Today was not the day to insist on something that had been distressing her so deeply for months. But what on earth was I going to do?' In the days that followed it became evident to my husband and me that we had a very real problem on our hands. *But if we are followers of Him, we do not walk alone, or in darkness!* With the Psalmist we can cry: "Hear, O Lord, and have mercy upon me: Lord, *be thou my helper.*" (Psalm 30v10). We could have used force in this situation - to the embarrassment of all concerned. However, I prayed in the days that followed... 'Lord, let *thy* will be done in this situation - not my will, my husband's will, or my daughter's will, but *thy will.*" The Lord's Prayer had never been more precious to me... "Thy will be done in earth, as it is in heaven..." (Matt. 6v9-13) As His child, I must commit every decision, every issue that I meet upon life's highway to Him. That week I telephoned the appropriate authorities, and discovered something that I had not fully realised before. Under the Irish constitution, provision has been made for 'home education,' and 'the family is acknowledged as the primary and natural educator of the child.' What concerned me most, though, was how I (an average mortal with no teaching experience) was supposed to fulfil the role of nine or ten teachers! 'A physical impossibility,' most people would say - but is not God 'the God of the impossible?' (Luke 1v37).

As I write, my daughter is still learning at home and (thankfully) she has just recently been legally registered after a visit from the Inspector. To say that I found that first week exhausting and challenging would be an understatement! Throughout it all, Susanna Wesley (1669-1742) came to mind. The mother of John Wesley, the great reformer and founder of the Methodist Church, and of his brother Charles Wesley, the great hymn writer, was the youngest in a family of twenty-five children. She herself gave birth to nineteen children. Only ten survived infancy and so she must have known her sorrows, but this wonderful mother sought to instil biblical principles into every subject that she taught her children. Sometimes we wonder about our children's' future, and their accomplishments on this earth, but is it not of more importance that their souls are destined for heaven? If they have trusted Him with their lives, then everything else will fall into place! "For this God is our God for ever and ever: he will be our guide even unto death." (Psalm 48v14).

He knows us much better than we know ourselves, and He knows well both our talents and limitations. What patience I lacked! The hymnist, Francis Ridley Havergal (1836-1879) also lacked patience with her pupils, but allowed the Lord to work wonderfully in her life. Because her short life was wholly dedicated to Christ, her inspired words will live on to bless and encourage generations of Christians for years to come. Often we may wonder why the calm, and reasonably smooth waters in our lives, suddenly become 'choppy.' Somehow, nothing is straightforward anymore and we begin to sink into anxiety. Peter miraculously walked on water to meet Jesus, but when he became intensely aware and anxious about that boisterous wind and water, he was filled with doubt that he could make it. It was at this point that he started to sink - because his heart was more aware of the prevailing conditions, than of Jesus' power to help him walk through the turbulence. (Matt. 14v25-31)

One night, after a long tiresome day of 'trying to be all things to all people,' I looked up at the great gentle light of the moon, as it emerged from wispy clouds in the night sky. 'Yes,' I thought, 'I must be positive in my Christian life. It is all too easy to be downcast and to see only the problems that surround me. I must *look up*, and keep my eyes upon Jesus - that "true Light which lighteth every man that cometh into the world. He was in the world, and the world was made by him, and the world knew him not." (John 1v9&10). The Creator of that great moon and stars is also my Lord and my Saviour - and the only One to whom I can unreservedly pour out my heart.' Just as Charles Wesley's spirit lay 'fast bound in sin and nature's night,' so did mine once. But the Lord has 'flamed the dungeon of my heart with light!' For this I thank "the Father of lights, with whom is no variableness, neither shadow of turning." (James 1v17) How marvellous it is to follow the Master and be led of His spirit, as I encounter the problems of life - today and every day. 'He will guide as to my daughter's education,' I thought. 'I must not be consumed with worry, and must trust Him, be led of His Word, and let Him work in my heart and life to help me be a better mother... in every sense of that word.'

Some day I shall look back on these events and know the reason why, but for now I can only trust my Saviour, keeping my eyes upon Him - not upon a seemingly impossible situation. Every turning point in our lives has a purpose, "and we know that all things work together for good to them that love God, to them who are the called according to his purpose." (Romans 8v28). My daughter works hard each day, steadily absorbing much interesting information – but of course education should encompass much more than this. In 1Cor. 8v1 we read: "...Knowledge puffeth up, but charity edifieth." A general medical practitioner may have immense knowledge but he can only be a good doctor, when that knowledge is combined with genuine compassion for the patients he is treating. Somehow the events in our History book, and those earthquakes and volcanoes in the Geography book take on a whole new meaning, when approached from a Christian perspective! As we labour to understand mathematical equations it is necessary to have *an interest*, otherwise the learning process would take forever! Surely it is even more wonderful, if we can but 'gain an interest in the Saviour's blood?' And the mysteries of Science pall into insignificance when compared with the great mystery that 'the Immortal died' - for you and me!

Charles Wesley's 'And Can It be...' is only one amongst six thousand, five hundred other hymns that he wrote in his lifetime. Behind he and his brother John (who preached the gospel fervently, and whose legacy continues through the centuries) there knelt a praying mother. I feel humbled when I read of her life, but He who 'flamed my dungeon with light,' wants me to trust Him for the hours, days, weeks and years that may lie ahead. Also, I must *look up to Him, not down*...at those turbulent waters. And He shall guide in my prayer life also... "Likewise the Spirit also helpeth our infirmities: for we know not what we should pray for as we ought: but the Spirit itself maketh intercession for us with groanings which cannot be uttered. And he that searcheth the hearts knoweth what is the mind of the Spirit, because he maketh intercession for the saints according to the will of God." (Romans 8v26&27). I remember simply praying... 'Thank you dear Lord, and please help me, for I have no help but thee.' Just as the sun broke through the mist that early September morning when I was overjoyed to find my daughter, the

Son of God wants to break through the mists and clouds of pain and worry which can potentially smother our every day lives - even as Christians. One morning I awoke to His simple message for me for that (and every) day. 'Keep your eyes upon me - not upon the passing problems of this life.' How lovely are the words of Prov. 4v18: "But the path of the just is as the shining light, that shineth more and more unto perfect day." More beautiful than the moon slipping through the night clouds, or the sun's shaft of warm new light, through September's morning mists, is the beauty of Jesus my Saviour and the light that He throws on my path on my daily walk with Him.

When young people are faced with the enormous choice of courses and careers that are presented to them, they may find it difficult to make the best decision. It is only when we know Jesus, as Saviour, Friend and Guide in this great maize of opportunity, that we can make the right decisions, and that those chains of sin, addiction, worry or confusion can be severed. Do you feel that you are drowning in life's troubles? My prayer is that you would simply cry out in the midst of those turbulent waters... "Lord, save me." (Matt. 14v30). Whether you are an anxious mother or father, a burdened businessman or a fearful student, He will hear and answer that cry for help. "And it shall come to pass, that whosoever shall call on the name of the Lord shall be saved." (Acts 2v21). How good it is to know that we need 'dread no condemnation,' when our feet are upon a path of faith - "that path of the just that shineth more and more unto perfect day." "Thou wilt shew me the path of life: in thy presence is fulness of joy; at thy right hand there are pleasures for evermore." (Psalm16v11).

114

The Path of the Just

Softly glowing light
Throughout the darkest night,
Every cloud its silver lining,
Every sorrow, love entwining.
My path meanders on,
In faith towards the Dawn -
Oh breaking glory, eternal Day,
Forever with my Lord to stay!

Autumn fields near Stamullen, Co. Meath.

(18)

"The Harvest Truly is Great, but the Labourers are Few..."
(Luke 10v2)

(September 16th - September30th)

In the small hours of an autumn night, I restlessly tossed, troubled, unable to sleep. Earlier that evening a great harvester had made its way up the narrow lane adjoining our field, and I could hear it droning on into the night. The high wind rushing through the leaves of the trees reminded me of those greater hurricanes, which had recently lashed the East Coast of America, leaving loss of life and widespread destruction in their wake. 'So many people dead - but what about their souls...? There are billions upon billions of souls on the face of the earth,' I thought, 'but how many Christians are doing anything at all to reach them?'

I thought about my own life. Most days were busy, very busy - but when do I speak a word for my Saviour? I started to think of people (some of them elderly) that I had known over the years. Their faces floated before me in the darkness, and I was troubled. For the most part they were respectable, friendly, church-going individuals... but they needed to see that only repentance and faith in the risen Saviour could save them. How difficult it is to reach the 'respectable!' Very often it is much easier for criminals who have been 'wallowing in the mud of great sin,' to see their need - than for law-abiding, church-going, charity workers, who believe that they are justified by their works. Most Christians find it difficult to present the gospel to 'respectable' loved ones and neighbours. To do so would risk hurtful confrontation, and perhaps embarrassment - but present the gospel, we must! Jesus said: "The harvest truly is great, but the labourers are few: pray ye therefore the Lord of the harvest, that he would send forth labourers into his harvest. Go your ways: behold, I send you forth as lambs among wolves." (Luke 10v2&3). If we profess to belong to Him, then this command (known as the 'great commission') is meant for us... "Go ye into all the world, and preach the gospel to every creature." (Mark 16v15).

116

"Go into all the world? How can *I* go into all the world?" A housebound, disabled person may exclaim. Yet, despite all obstacles, the Lord has strategic places throughout His great vineyard for those who are led of His spirit! Also, if we ask for opportunities to be presented to us, He will certainly answer such a prayer! Indeed, some of us *may* be called to work in far-flung nations of the world (and those locations may change with circumstance) - but not one of us is free from 'the great commission.' Often in our lives, you or I may be the only Christian witness available to certain souls, but it is important to remember that our witness can only be effective if we are *blameless* subjects of His Kingdom. Actions often speak louder than words and we are being watched closely by those who do not know the Saviour, but who (rightly) expect a very high standard from the professing Christian. David indicates in Psalm 51v12&13 that he cannot be of use to the Lord, until his sin is dealt with... *"Then* will I teach transgressors thy ways; and sinners shall be converted unto thee."

One of the signs that there is something wrong with our relationship with the Saviour is when we have no desire to witness for Him, and to see souls saved. "No man, when he hath lighted a candle, putteth it in a secret place, neither under a bushel, but on a candlestick, that they which come in may see the light. The light of the body is the eye: therefore when thine eye is single, thy whole body also is full of light; but when thine eye is evil, thy body also is full of darkness. Take heed therefore that the light which is in thee be not darkness. If thy whole body therefore be full of light, having no part dark, the whole shall be full of light, as when the bright shining of a candle doth give thee light." (Luke 11v33-36).

We are all different in personality, it is true, but the Lord can use even the most shy, timid person to draw souls to himself. We may be afraid to approach that formidable 'pillar of society' or that celebrity with the gospel; but if we go by faith, He will show us when and how this can be done. Sometimes He does this in amazing ways. Jesus is our marvellous example, as the Greatest Soul Winner ever. He had that wonderful way of starting a conversation, at a wavelength suitable to the individual He was reaching out to. 'The woman at the well,' is a classic example of this. "Give me to drink," Jesus asks her in John 4v7. She (knowing that He is a Jew) is amazed that He has any dealings with her, a Samaritan. Sometimes, too, an individual may be surprised when we address our conversation to them. Perhaps the person may see us as being on a different social (or other level) to themselves. However, when His love for souls fills our hearts, He will break down every barrier for… "There is no fear in love; but perfect love casteth out fear: because fear hath torment. He that feareth is not made perfect in love." (1John 4v18). Also, "there is no difference between the Jew and the Greek: for the same Lord over all is rich unto all that call upon him." (Rom. 10v12).

Jesus soon turned the woman's attention to an even more important issue than our basic need for water… "If thou knewest the gift of God, and who it is that saith to thee, Give me to drink: thou wouldst have asked of him, and he would have given thee living water." (John 4v10). When He asks her to bring her husband to Him, she replies that she has no husband. Jesus then reveals His omniscience in verses 17&18… "Thou hast well said, I have no husband: For thou hast had five husbands; and he whom thou now hast is not thy husband: in that saidst thou truly." Unlike Jesus, we may not know the life-story of the person we are speaking to, although a troubled soul may wish to confide in us. Our world is currently full of souls like that Samaritan woman, and how the Saviour wants to touch those lives, to heal the broken-hearted, and to open the eyes of the spiritually blind! "And I will bring the blind by a way that they knew not; I will lead them in paths that they have not known: I will make darkness light before them, and crooked things straight. These things will I do unto them, and not forsake them." (Isaiah 42v16). But He needs ambassadors!

That Samaritan woman, having believed, proceeded to spread the news to her neighbours… "And many of the Samaritans of that city believed on him for the sayings of the woman, which testified, He told me all that ever I did." (John 4v39). In Rom. 10v9-11, we read: "That if thou shalt confess with thy mouth the Lord Jesus, and shalt believe in thine heart that God hath raised him from the dead, thou shalt be saved. For with the heart man believeth unto righteousness; and with the mouth confession is made unto salvation. For the scripture saith, Whosoever believeth on him shall not be ashamed." In Verse 10 we see that confession is necessary for very salvation!

Furthermore we read in Matthew 10v32&33... "Whosoever therefore shall confess before men, him will I confess also before my Father which is in heaven. But whosoever shall deny me before men, him will I also deny before my Father which is in heaven."

Everything shall be made manifest on that Great Day, referred to in Rev. 14v15... "Thrust in thy sickle, and reap: for the time is come for thee to reap; for the harvest of the earth is ripe." At this moment (whatever our situation or location, as Christians) the Lord commands us to reach the lost around us. Those of our own households or our neighbours may present the greatest challenge of all! "How then shall they call on him in whom they have not believed? And how shall they believe in him of whom they have not heard? And how shall they hear without a preacher? And how shall they preach, except they be sent? As it is written, How beautiful are the feet of them that preach the gospel of peace, and bring glad tidings of good things!" (Rom. 10v14&15).

On that sleepless night, my thoughts travelled back to the spring of the year. My husband and I, along with dozens of other Christians, had gathered for a farewell service, for a young couple and their four children, who were going to work for the Lord in Armenia. The marquee, which was erected for the occasion in a field, was filled with hymns, prayers and appropriate words for the occasion. Having previously seen slides of living conditions in that impoverished country, I remember looking at the children of the family, and feeling really sorry for them. 'What a culture shock!' I thought. That night their young faces and those of their parents filled my thoughts, and I prayed for them. How the Lord rewards those who labour for Him! "And every one that hath forsaken houses, or brethren, or sisters, or father, or mother, or wife, or children, or lands, for my name's sake, shall receive an hundredfold, and shall inherit eternal life." (Matt. 19v29)

'But what are these among so many...? Not enough workers, not enough tracts...' My jumbled thoughts on the verge of sleep were dwelling on yet another time, another place... One afternoon, some years previously, I had overheard a conversation between two ladies in a charity shop. "They're bringing the relics of St. Theresa to the monastery. Are you going?" At this I pricked up my ears, because the monastery in question was close to where I lived. Driving home,

I thought: 'what an opportunity! There will be dozens of people there. Perhaps I could give out copies of a priest's testimony'... And so, to work - the local office bureau made a lot of money from photocopies that day! However, the great evening arrived, and I was absolutely terrified. Taking one look at the hundreds (not dozens) of people who were queuing to see the relics, and then at my feeble few leaflets, I felt like running away! Instead, I prayed, took a deep breath, and started to distribute them. Initially I had received smiles of approval and thanks, from those who had just received their leaflets. (Possibly they thought that I was connected with the event.) Then I began to hear muttering from those who had had an opportunity to read their leaflets, from further back in the queue. Despite this, not one was dropped to the ground, and only eternity shall reveal the outcome. My only regret is that so few of the people got one.

Those hundreds of people that I saw reminded me of the following verses in Joel 3v14&15: "Multitudes, multitudes in the valley of decision: for the day of the Lord is near in the valley of decision. The sun and the moon shall be darkened, and the stars shall withdraw their shining." At dusk I had watched the harvester at work, and had been reminded of how much harvesting has changed over the years. Somehow those beaming lights shone more brightly, as darkness descended! One thing remains constant, though, for we still have those 'tares amongst the wheat.' (Matt. 13v38). Jesus explains His parable in Matthew 13v37-43. "He that soweth the good seed is the Son of man; The field is the world; the good seed are the children of the kingdom; but the tares are the children of the wicked one; The enemy that sowed them is the devil; the harvest is the end of the world; and the reapers are the angels..." (Verses37-39) In verse 43 we read: "Then shall the righteous shine forth as the sun in the kingdom of their Father. Who hath ears to hear, let him hear."

Are you ready for that Great Harvest? At present the 'tares and the wheat' grow together in our world, but some day there will be a separation. Jesus said: "Let both grow together until the harvest: and in the time of harvest I will say to the reapers, Gather ye together first the tares, and bind them in bundles to burn them: but gather the wheat into my barn." (Matt. 13v30). The alternative to the 'barn' (or the safety of heaven) is unthinkable. John the Baptist said… "I indeed baptize you with water unto repentance: but he that cometh after me is mightier than I, whose shoes I am not worthy to bear: he shall baptize you with the Holy Ghost, and with fire: Whose fan is in his hand, and he will throughly purge his floor, and gather his wheat into the garner; but he will burn up the chaff with unquenchable fire." (Matt. 3v11&12).

The 'day of the Lord' is near in 'the valley of decision.' This then is the sombre question for each soul upon the earth… 'Will you be numbered with the wheat - or with the tares?' Note Joshua's exhortation in Joshua 24v15… "choose you this day whom ye will serve;" God forbid that we should hear these words… "Depart from me, ye cursed, into everlasting fire, prepared for the devil and his angels…" (Matt. 25v41). Indeed the lake of fire *was* prepared for the devil and his angels; it was never God's will that members of the human race (who were made in His image and for whom the blood of the Lord Jesus Christ was shed) should go there. I remember once being convicted by that verse… "The harvest is past, the summer is ended, and we are not saved." (Jer. 8v20). But praise God that I decided to follow Him, and am no longer numbered with the tares. Prior to my conversion, I remember also being troubled and confused by the words of someone who said that we had no control over our own destinies, and that God had pre-destined all souls into either eternal bliss in heaven - or eternal suffering in hell. For a short time I seriously thought that I may be one of those who were 'predestined to go to hell.' This filled me with an indescribable bleak helplessness, until the Lord opened my eyes.

God, because He is omniscient, naturally knows the path that each one of us will take - yes, even before the foundation of the world. Therefore… "For whom he did foreknow, he also did predestinate to be conformed to the image of his Son, that he might be the firstborn among many brethren. Moreover whom he did predestinate, them he also called: and whom he called, them he also justified: and whom he justified, them he also glorified." (Rom. 8v29&30). Here we may see clearly that those whom He foreknew who would *choose* to follow Him, and *endure unto the end* (Matt.10v22), are predestined to be conformed to the image of His Son. Since His blood avails for all (1John 2v2; 1Tim. 2v6; 2Cor

5v14&15), it is His will that all should come to repentance in Him, and that none should perish (2Pet. 3v9). If people perish, it is because they have chosen the "broad road that leads to destruction" (Matt. 7v13) - not because they have been pre-destined to eternal destruction. Nowhere in God's Word are we told that we have no control over our own destinies! Furthermore, how can His ambassadors be effective in their work and witness, when they have (at the back of their minds) a conception that the eternal destinies of all souls have been foreordained?

As I tossed, unable to sleep that night, I longed that the whole world of men and women and boys and girls, would see the goodness of the Lord who gave His only begotten Son - and not only see, but repent, and trust Him for salvation. "For the Son of man is not come to destroy men's lives, but to save them..." (Luke 9v56). To the Christian He says: "Say not ye, There are yet four months, and then cometh harvest? Behold I say unto you, Lift up your eyes, and look on the fields; for they are white already to harvest. And he that reapeth receiveth wages, and gathereth fruit unto life eternal: that both he that soweth and he that reapeth may rejoice together. And herein is that saying true, One soweth, and another reapeth. I sent you to reap that whereon ye bestowed no labour: other men laboured, and ye are entered into their labours." (John 4v35-38). He has work for you and me to do, while it is 'day.' Great harvesters work steadily for long hours, so that costly sheaves of golden grain may be safely gathered into the storehouse. Oh that our lives would be burned out in His service, and that we could say with the apostle Paul... "For to me to live is Christ, and to die is gain." (Phil. 1v21) To God be the glory.

I saw a field of harvest gold,
Before the sun was set,
Each precious ear, a story told,
But the work is waiting yet.
O come with me, my Christian friend,
And let us work where he doth send,
For shadows grow, as night draws on,
And souls may die before the Dawn.

(Luke 10v2)

In the Stamullen countryside, Co. Meath.

(19)

"Ever Learning" …
(2 Tim. 3v7)

(October 1st - October 15th)

My eldest daughter burst in through the back door, her face flushed and damp with the autumn wind and rain. "Well, how did your first day in the new course go, and what are your classmates like?" I queried, while preparing the evening meal.
"Oh Mum," she yawned, flopping into an armchair, "I'm exhausted! You wouldn't believe it - some of them are even older than *you!*"
"Really?" I said, raising my eyebrows.
"Oh, *much* older - some of them look like they're retired."
"Well," I said, with a smile, "good for them. It's a great idea to keep exercising the old brain. Stops it from going rusty!"
I remembered the prospectus (one of many) that we had scrutinized recently. "Learning is a life-long process" it had said. Indeed, this new philosophy of "education for life" is beginning to take hold in our society, so that it is possible to learn a new skill, discover a hidden talent or successfully complete a degree course at any time in our lives. A few weeks after my daughter's first encounter with her new course, the postman was standing outside our door with a fat parcel, containing the first section of a correspondence course. On the cover was printed the following:

"I am still learning"
Michelangelo 1475- 1564

While some inhabitants (especially women) in distant lands receive little or no education, our system recommends a 'certain minimum education' for all until the age of sixteen. After that we may choose to continue further study (as finances and circumstances will allow) for many years, at second, and then third level institutions. Post-graduate studies and further research may continue until retirement - and beyond! With the onslaught of darker evenings and the fall of autumn leaves, citizens (young and old) browse eagerly through their local guide to night classes. Ambitions large and small may be fulfilled and the lost opportunities of youth recouped, as every subject 'under the sun' is available.

I remember well my first day at school and I have to say that it was never my favourite place over the years! In those days teachers were the ultimate disciplinarians and education was not presented in a very attractive light. Being a shy, sensitive child I was never at the forefront of activities and often a victim of bullying. Nowadays, with awareness of the latter and a more child-centred environment, education can be an enjoyable and fulfilling experience for all - although I do sometimes feel sorry for the teachers! As children we feared most of them, but I can remember those whose encouraging words still enrich my life today - and to whom I shall ever be grateful. Examinations, however, were my downfall, and rarely an indication of my performance during the year. I shall never forget the one which I sat directly after the death of a school friend, of whom I was very fond. She had been involved in a car accident in which her sister and cousin had also died. It was a traumatic time and our whole class had attended the funeral. Tears blinded my eyes in the stifling atmosphere of the great examination hall. She was the first dead person I had ever seen and I could think of nothing else but her pale young face, eyes closed to this world forever. Not surprisingly, I failed miserably.

Nevertheless, though we may fail in the affairs of this world, how wonderful is the knowledge that we do not require a certificate, diploma, degree or PhD. to enter the gates of Heaven! In Acts 4v13 we read: "Now when they saw the boldness of Peter and John, and perceived that they were unlearned and ignorant men, they marvelled; and they took knowledge of them, that they had been with Jesus." Nowadays, to be an established minister of religion, one is required to have substantial qualifications, and yet we learn in 1Cor. 1v17-21: "For Christ sent me not to baptize, but to preach the gospel: not with wisdom of words, lest the cross of Christ should be made of non effect. For the preaching of the cross is to them that perish foolishness; but unto us which are saved it is the power of God. For it is written, I will destroy the wisdom of the wise, and will bring to nothing the understanding of the prudent. Where is the wise? where is the scribe? where is the disputer of this world? hath not God made foolish the wisdom of this world? For after that in the wisdom of God the world by wisdom knew not God, it pleased God by the foolishness of preaching to save them that believe." I believe it is true to say, that just as it was in the days of the apostles, so it is today - for there are unlearned men of humble occupations and backgrounds who fruitfully preach "Christ crucified, unto the Jews a stumbling block, and unto the Greeks foolishness..." (1 Cor. 1v23).

In 1Cor. 1v26 we learn that... "not many wise men after the flesh, not many mighty, not many noble, are called:" I can recall feeling like 'a fish out of water' when attending a ceremony in a third level institution. That atmosphere of pomp, the ceremonial gowns and the sea of faces – included those who were so proud of their own intellect! Some day we will stand before God, devoid of all the trappings of this life, for our intellectual achievements are nothing to Him. However, if we are Christians, He will expect us to have used the diverse talents and gifts (which He has given each one of us) for His glory. In Eccl. 9v10 we read: "Whatsoever thy hand findeth to do, do it with thy might; for there is no work, nor device, nor knowledge, nor wisdom, in the grave, whither thou goest." Whatever our circumstances in this life (and regardless of age/disability/lack of previous education/or social background) each one of us is unique in His sight, although not all of us are 'swots!' The amazing life of Gladys Aylward touched the hearts of millions, but only because she kept her eyes on the Saviour, and refused to be deterred by lack of education, financial support - or even physical danger. The humble little parlour maid, born in 1902, and famous for her missionary work in war-torn China (especially amongst children) is surely an example of how God "hath chosen the weak things of the world to confound the things which are mighty;" (1 Cor. 1v27). If there is a language to be learned, a mountain to be trekked or an instrument to be played, so that we can be useful servants of the King in today's world, He will assist us - providing that our course of action is totally within His will. Even if we are lying on a hospital bed, unable to move a muscle, we can achieve the most important job of all as Christians - for we can *pray!* Herein lies the secret behind all great battles won for the King.

In 1 Tim. 4v14 Paul tells Timothy: "Neglect not the gift that is in thee, which was given thee by prophecy, with the laying on of the hands of the presbytery." And again, in 2Tim.1v6&7 he reminds Timothy of these very words, adding…"For God hath not given us the spirit of fear; but of power, and of love, and of a sound mind." Indeed love, that love which desires to see our fellowmen saved, and God glorified, must be the driving force behind our earthly endeavours. The Lord needs His people everywhere - and often He leads us down unconventional avenues, but we must be prepared to go where He wants us to go, and do what He wants us to do.

Above all else, we must study His Word, the Bible. "Study to shew thyself approved unto God, a workman that needeth not to be ashamed, rightly dividing the word of truth," Paul tells Timothy in 2Tim. 2v15. The Word of God must be the primary and single great influence behind every decision we make about our future. Also, we must never hold education in such high esteem, that we forget to acknowledge the Creator of all knowledge. In theory, education should be a civilising influence and to our advantage, but without Christ it can produce obnoxiously proud, self-sufficient people who care little for their fellowmen.

Paul, in his second epistle to Timothy, in chapter 3, lists the traits of those who shall live in the last days, and in verse 7 we learn that there will be those who are … "Ever learning, and never able to come to the knowledge of the truth." One morning I switched on the radio, and instead of the news (which I wanted to hear) a booming voice uttered these words: "Educate! Educate! Educate! This is the solution to a civilised society!" "What rubbish," I muttered, thinking of a recent incident where some well-educated young men from a posh school, had kicked another young man to death outside one of Dublin's nightclubs. This was not, unfortunately, an isolated incident. Disregard for human life is on the increase - an embarrassing feature in a society where educational standards are amongst the highest in the world.

Are you involved in education - either as a teacher, or student? If you are a Christian - let God use your skills to His glory, and be prepared to work hard, with honesty and dedication in the field which He has chosen for you, so that you may positively influence the lives of others. As a couple of apt lines from Frances Ridley Havergal's hymn "Take my Life" goes:

"Take my intellect, and use
Ev'ry power as Thou shalt choose."

If you are not a Christian, remember that intellectual (or any other achievement) is no passport to heaven. Or is it that you wish to serve Him, but feel that your education is inadequate?   Be encouraged, for His word tells us: "For ye see your calling, brethren, how that not many wise men after the flesh, not many mighty, not many noble, are called: But God hath chosen the foolish things of the world to confound the wise; and God hath chosen the weak things of the world to confound the things which are mighty; And base things of the world; and things which are despised, hath God chosen, yea, and things which are not, to bring to nought things that are: That *no flesh should glory in His presence.* But of him are ye in Christ Jesus, who of God is made unto us wisdom, and righteousness, and sanctification, and redemption: That, according as it is written, He that glorieth, let him glory in the Lord." (1 Cor. 1v26-31).

If the battle is the Lord's,
Then what have we to fear?
Cast off thine heavy armour -
He saveth not with sword or spear!

The Lord shall fight for you,
And ye shall hold your peace,
Though chariots pursue
And enemies increase!

For He hath chosen the weak,
And that which men despise,
To bring to naught the mighty,
To confound the great and wise!

The "Long Room," an old library in Trinity College, Dublin, containing over 250,000 books.

20

The Spirit of Good and the Spirit of Evil
(1John 4v1-4)

(16th October - 31st October)

The night was almost pitch black, and a heavy odour of fireworks hung in the cold air after the rain shower. Stealthily we made our way down the narrow lane and onwards, until we came to my uncle's house and apple farm. A faint half moon now slipped through the clouds, and every stark tree in the misty orchard seemed to cast eerie shadows on the cold earth. "What shall we do here?" someone murmured.

"Let's pile up some empty apple boxes against their front door, then ring the doorbell and scarper!" Came a whispered suggestion, "and when they come to the door... hey presto! The lot will fall." Swiftly and silently we piled up the empty boxes, and then ran behind some trees - or perhaps it was a wall. To be honest it is so long ago, that I can't remember which! From the safety of our hide-out we watched the proceedings, while one of our 'brave' company volunteered to ring the doorbell. He ran swiftly back to us, and we watched in amusement as my poor uncle opened the door, and the boxes noisily collapsed in all directions. Somehow, though, as we left the scene I felt a little tinge of sorrow, and regret...

Running quietly from that house, we moved on to our next 'victims.' I was the only girl in the gang, and for me Halloween night was one of the most exciting times of the year. Shortly we came to another country house, where the washing still hung damply in the cold night air. "Let's take Mrs. M.'s washing and put it everywhere," whispered someone. At this I had had enough. Apple boxes against a door were bad enough, but being a girl and the eldest in the family, I appreciated how difficult it was to get washing dry in those days. "No!" I shouted vehemently, "I'm having nothing to do with this one. That's not fair!" Somehow the excitement had 'gone sour.' Leaving the rest of the gang (who were now angry with me for raising my voice) I walked quickly towards our long narrow lane - and home. I was alone now and the night seemed to envelop me in its dark cloak. Familiar objects took on a sinister shape in the light of the faint moon. Was that really the wooden gate, or was it the entrance to something more terrible than the green meadow? A tree's gnarled branches clawing at the dilapidated tin shed startled me, but now thankfully I could see the warm lights of our old white-washed home and I ran downhill that last little bit of the journey.

Bursting through our front (and only) door, I ran towards the little living room which was full of adults and my two younger sisters. Two aunts and an uncle sat cracking nuts around the flickering log fire, while my father chatted away and my mother came in from the scullery, carrying numerous generous helpings of apple crumble and custard. "Ah! Just in time!" She greeted me with her motherly smile and then turned towards the door, where my brother and others were standing, their faces glowing innocently after their outdoor activities on that cold October night. On into that night we were to hear the soaring whistle of all types of fireworks, which illuminated the dark autumn sky with their splendour.

Such was our traditional Halloween night in that rural part of Northern Ireland where I lived as a child. On reflection, I have still fond memories of the 'get-togethers' - those nights around the fireside with their laughter and warmth, but the mischievous feats that were (and still are) a part of traditional Halloween in many areas, hold no attraction for me now. Is it because I have grown older and a bit 'stuffy?' No, I believe that it is because I can now see, as a Christian, a different side to this traditional Irish holiday - one which holds great dread for some.

Very recently I met an elderly acquaintance on the streets of a local town, which is close to my current home in Co. Meath. "Oh, how I hate this time of the year!" she told me. "They bang my door and run away, and then there's the noise of fireworks until all hours of the morning. All the dogs around are barking and terrified."

"It must be awful for you," I sympathised with her. "We have no trouble like that where we live now, but I remember how it was when we lived here..." I had no sooner finished my words, than my thoughts turned to something which my husband had witnessed early one morning - something which had troubled me at the time. Apart from the usual activities of fireworks and mischief, there are other, very horrific, proceedings which occur on this night in many places throughout the world. This is the night when animals (and sometimes even human beings) are sacrificed to the devil. We have only to read the testimonies of those who were once involved deeply in the occult, to realise that this is not mere sensationalism. That such practices occur in Ireland, I have no doubt. Some years ago my husband was rushing to work very early in the morning, when he discovered, en route, the remains of an unidentifiable animal, which looked like it had been used for sacrificial purposes on the previous night. More recently I have had suspicions that our local megalithic tomb is being used as something more than a sight-seeing rendezvous of historical significance.

Never has Halloween been as popular and commercialised as it is today, and never have those who worship the devil had such freedom to exercise their 'crafts.' While the witches in bygone days were clandestine in their operations, because of the fear of being put to death, witches nowadays do television interviews and are open about their 'craft.' In Galatians 5v19-21, we read: "Now the works of the flesh are manifest, which are these; Adultery, fornication, uncleanness, lasciviousness, Idolatry, witchcraft, hatred, variance, emulations, wrath, strife, seditions, heresies, Envyings, murders, drunkenness, revellings, and such like: of the which I tell you before, as I have also told you in time past, that they which do such things shall not inherit the kingdom of God."

The popular image of a witch or wizard, as portrayed in children's story books is a far cry from current reality! Witches, far from being malicious old hags, brandishing a broomstick in one hand and stirring a cauldron with the other, come in many guises these days. The occult in general, operates under many different labels - some of them seemingly harmless. As Christians, we don't need to know the full details concerning each and every single ploy of the devil, but we *do* need to walk closely with the Lord and to constantly ask Him for discernment and protection. "Be sober, be vigilant; because your adversary the devil, as a roaring lion, walketh about, seeking whom he may devour." (1Pet. 5v8)

Numerous superstitious practices which are familiar to the Irish (and possibly many other countries in the world) are denigrated in God's Word. Most secular newspapers and magazines nowadays have a column devoted to astrology - once a practice in ancient

Babylon. In Isaiah 47v13&14 we read: "Thou art wearied in the multitude of thy counsels. Let now the astrologers, the stargazers, the monthly prognosticators, stand up, and save thee from these things which shall come upon thee. Behold, they shall be as stubble; the fire shall burn them; they shall not deliver themselves from the power of the flame: there shall not be a coal to warm at, nor fire to sit before it."

Mention of fire itself, reminds me of the familiar bonfires we see on Halloween night. Many are unaware that this is an old Pagan practice, and while the thinking behind most 'bonfires' is harmless as such, there is a return to the "*bone*fire," and other clandestine evil rituals in our society - not only on Halloween night. Clairvoyance is one practice which is certainly not clandestine in operation. Psychics and mediums now frequent our airwaves, displaying their supernatural abilities - which have also been used in a bid to locate missing persons. Fortune-Tellers (who predict the future by various means) are perhaps even *more* common than their occultist sisters. In 1Samuel 28v3 we read... "Now Samuel was dead, and all Israel had lamented him in Ramah, even in his own city. And Saul had put away those that had familiar spirits, and the wizards, out of the land." However, Saul's actions (pertaining to David) displeased God, and so He was not with him in his battles. If God is not with us, we are fighting 'a losing battle!' Often when this happens, people will inevitably turn to that other inferior source of power - the devil, and all his devices. Having put away those with 'familiar spirits,' Saul in his moment of crises turns around and says... "Seek me a woman that hath a familiar spirit, that I may go to her, and inquire of her." (1Samuel 28v7) We learn how the witch of En-dor conjured up 'Samuel' for the benefit of Saul - but was it Samuel?

Distressed souls often call upon clairvoyants to help them to regain contact with loved ones who have died, but God's Word clearly states that there can be *no* contact with those who have passed away from this life. Since God condemns that which was practised by the Witch of En-dor, we have no reason to believe that the spirit is Samuel's. In 1Chron. 10v13 we learn that it was Saul's consultation with the witch that partially contributed to his downfall... "So Saul died for his transgression which he committed against the Lord, even against the word of the Lord, which he kept not, and also for asking counsel of one that had a familiar spirit, to inquire of it;" The devil specializes in producing evil spirits - to tell us what we want (or don't want) to hear. As a fallen angel who knows scripture well, of course he has access to some information about the future! In Hebrews 9v27 we learn that... "it is appointed unto man once to die, but after this the judgement." When the soul of man leaves his body after death, its eternal destiny is in either of two places - Heaven or Hell. No other place is mentioned in the Bible. In Luke 16v19-31, where we read the account of Lazarus and the rich man, we may see clearly that there is a "great gulf fixed: so that they which would pass from hence to you cannot; neither can they pass to us, that would come from thence." (Verse 26). In Verse 24 we read that the rich man cried: "Father Abraham, have mercy on me, and send Lazarus, that he may dip the tip of his finger in water, and cool my tongue; for I am tormented in this flame." It is interesting to note that while the rich man was able to see Lazarus in Abraham's bosom, and indeed there was dialogue between himself and Abraham, we are not told that Lazarus was aware of the torment of the rich man. The latter, concerned for his brothers who are still alive on the earth, asks that Lazarus be sent to them as a witness - but neither can this be granted... "And he said unto him, If they hear not Moses and the prophets, neither will they be persuaded, though one rose from the dead..." (Verse 31). How important it is, then, to make sure that we are right with God in this life, in order that we may have hope for our own souls in eternity – and be an effective witness to our loved ones! It is only through the power of the risen Saviour that our lives can change, our minds and bodies are healed – and that those demons which would seek to destroy us, may be cast out.

In Matthew 8v28, we read that Jesus met "two possessed with devils, coming out of the tombs, exceeding fierce, so that no man might pass by that way." Those devils knew Jesus immediately! "What have we to do with thee, Jesus, thou Son of God? Art thou come hither to torment us before the time?" (Verse 29). In Verse 31, these demons ask... "If thou cast us out, suffer us to go away into the herd of swine." Then there is the familiar account in Verse 32 of how "the whole herd of swine ran violently down a steep place into the sea, and perished in the waters." What tremendous peace those two previously possessed souls must have had, and how marvellous that in the name of Jesus - demons must flee!

In 1John 4v4, Christians are reassured... "Ye are of God, little children, and have overcome them: because greater is he that is in you, than he that is in the world." Some day (perhaps sooner than we think) the devil, and all his army of evil spirits will be "cast into the lake of fire and brimstone, where the beast and the false prophet *are*, and shall be tormented day and night for ever and ever." (Rev. 20v10). Meanwhile we must take refuge in the Lord our Saviour, whose blood has conquered all... "And then shall that Wicked be revealed, whom the Lord shall consume with the spirit of his mouth, and shall destroy with the brightness of his coming:" (2Thess. 2v8) In Deuteronomy 18v10-12 the Lord commands His people... "There shall not be found among you any one that maketh his son or his daughter to pass through the fire, or that useth divination, or an observer of times, or an enchanter, or a witch. Or a charmer, or a consulter with familiar spirits, or a wizard, or a necromancer. For all that do these things are an abomination unto the Lord: and because of these abominations the Lord thy God doth drive them out before thee." Our world, our neighbourhood, is currently full of superstitious rites, magic, spiritualist practices and 'therapies' of dubious origin, all of which are condemned in God's Word. At some otherwise harmless events, such as craft fairs one will more than likely find a fortune teller, someone selling 'Angel Cards,' or some 'New Age' related articles or literature for sale. "Psychics" advertising in newspapers claim to offer "peace of mind, and assurance." Surely we should be aware, as Christians, that there is a great turning away to the evil things of darkness, in the age in which we live?

One cold autumn evening while out walking close to our County Meath home, we discovered yet another megalithic tomb. We had suspected its existence for some time, but now we stood in the fading light trying to read an old and rusting Department of Environment notice. Obviously no attempt had been made to excavate the tomb. In the twilight I stood for a while watching darkness fall around this ancient place where Neolithic people had buried their cremated dead. As the great mound, and the trees surrounding it became dark silhouettes against the night sky, I wondered about these people who lived thousands of years before Christ. They had had their ancient rituals - but what of the souls of those who had never heard of our Lord and Saviour, Jesus Christ? As the wind whispered in the trees around me, I suddenly remembered some words from Genesis 18v25... "Shall not the Judge of all the earth do right?" They may have lived out their lives, ignorant of God's grace to all mankind - but their destiny is in His hands. My concern must not be for those whose destinies are in the hands of a righteous and loving God - but rather to reach the living. Many, even today, live in superstition having never understood the simple truth of the gospel by which we must be saved. "For Christ also hath once suffered for sins, the just for the unjust, that he might bring us to God, being put to death in the flesh, but quickened by the Spirit:" (1Peter 3v18).

"And the times of this ignorance God winked at; but now commandeth all men every where to repent." (Acts 17v30). There is no excuse for those who have heard the glorious message of salvation. Jesus says of those who reject the gospel... "Verily I say unto you, It shall be more tolerable for the Land of Sodom and Go-mor-rha in the day of judgement, than for that city." (Matt. 10v15) In John 8v36 we learn: "If the Son therefore shall make you free, ye shall be free indeed." Free from superstition, free from every entanglement and snare of the evil one! There is no demon that He cannot cast out, and there is no bad spirit that He cannot put to flight, but those who are afflicted in such a way must be willing for the work of the loving Saviour in their hearts. "This then is the message which we have heard of him, and declare unto you, that God is light, and in him is no darkness at all." (1John 1v5) Let us therefore, as Christians, not celebrate the works of darkness - even if they are cloaked in seemingly harmless well-known traditions.

It was on 31st October, 1517, on the eve of a "traditional religious celebration," that Martin Luther nailed his Ninety-five Theses to the church door. Perhaps a celebration of the great truths of the Reformation would be more appropriate on this date? The following verses are surely at variance with many of those pranks on Halloween night... "Love worketh no ill to his neighbour: therefore love is the fulfilling of the law. And that, knowing the time, that now it is high time to awake out of sleep: for now is our salvation nearer than when we believed. The night is far spent, the day is at hand: let us therefore cast off the works of darkness, and let us put on the armour of light." (Romans 13v10-12) Perhaps you feel that you *do* abhor those "works of darkness," but have never trusted the Living Saviour. Why not trust Him now? God forbid that you should spend eternity with those who are described in Rev. 21v8… "But the fearful, and unbelieving, and the abominable, and murderers, and whoremongers, and sorcerers, and idolaters, and all liars, shall have their part in the lake which burneth with fire and brimstone: which is the second death." The Saviour's will is that you would be numbered with those who have overcome the evil one "by the blood of the Lamb, and by the word of their testimony; and they loved not their lives unto death" (Rev. 12v11). A number of years after that Halloween night (and many years ago now) I gave my life to the Lord, as a young adult of twenty-five. Now with the redeemed I can say: "Giving thanks unto the Father, which hath made us meet to be partakers of the inheritance of the saints in light: Who hath delivered us from the power of darkness, and hath translated us into the kingdom of his dear Son: In whom we have redemption, through his blood, even the forgiveness of sins:" (Col. 1v12-14) Oh that all who read would claim these promises, cast off the works of darkness (in *His* strength) and believe in the Lord Jesus Christ for salvation. "For we wrestle not against flesh and blood, but against principalities, against powers, against the rulers of the darkness of this world, against spiritual wickedness in high places." (Eph.6v12)

Greater Is He That Is In You...
(1John4v4)

He healed the sick and raised the dead,
He made the blind to see,
And in His name the demons fled,
And drowned within the sea.

He walked upon the stormy wave,
And bid the wind to cease,
He rose in triumph from the grave,
And lives to give us peace.

So what have we to fear from he,
Who walketh here below,
If deep within our hearts lives He...
Who has conquered every foe?

Tower and graves, Glendalough, Co. Wicklow.

21

Wars, Rumours of War, Three Hostages… and the Prayers of the
Saints
(Matthew 21v22 & Matthew 24v6-8)

(1st November - 15th November)

Whilst driving to my Co. Meath home at dusk one evening in the late autumn of 2004, I switched the radio on for news. It was approaching that time of the year when the dead of two world wars are remembered, and poppies (redder than the setting sun that evening) are worn by many in remembrance of those who "shall grow not old, as we that are left grow old…" The voice on the radio was telling me of alarming casualties in Iraq and problems in Afghanistan, in the wake of their recent elections. Then, in the midst of it all a familiar name rang out - that of a young woman who had been a school friend of my younger sister many years ago. My old village of Richhill, nestling in the 'Orchard County' of Armagh was also mentioned. Open-mouthed with shock, I switched the radio off, my mind travelling back the years to happy childhood days. Memories of a birthday party, children's laughter… yes, I remembered Annetta. Now I could scarcely believe the terrible thing that had happened, for (along with two others) she had been taken hostage in the Afghan capital, Kabul.

My initial shock was replaced by a feeling of dread, for I had been aware of the recent news of those who had been mercilessly beheaded in neighbouring Iraq. From the moment that I heard this shocking news, the Lord burdened me to pray for Annetta, her fellow hostages (from Kosovo and the Philippines) and their loved ones. My youngest daughter, who was the only one with me in the car at the time, asked: "What's wrong Mum? Do you know this person?"

"Yes," I replied, "I remember her from a long time ago. Now she is in a very dangerous situation, and desperately needs prayer."

In the weeks that followed, prayer was my constant companion - night and day. Why did I feel so burdened for someone whom I had not seen in many years, and of whose life I knew little of now? I believe that the Lord placed that burden there - and He burdened many other Christians too. I contacted all of the Christians with whom I was acquainted locally, and they assured me that they too, would pray. Often I would be awakened in the 'small hours' of the morning, in the knowledge that those involved in this situation needed much fervent prayer. I would think of Annetta, perhaps somewhere alone in a dark, desolate room, held captive - maybe hungry, cold and terrified. Their captors had said that they had the wherewithal to hold them for months, even years, until their demands were met. Those demands (including the release of Taliban prisoners in Guntanamo Bay, Cuba) seemed unreasonable, almost impossible. Then I would think of the relatives of those held - sick with worry and dread, and dearly wanting to have their loved ones alive and with them once more.

In Annetta's native village of Richhill many Christians gathered for prayer at all times of the day and evening. It must be said that the Lord only hears those who are His servants: those who have been truly born again of the Spirit of God, and who are walking with Him. "Now we know that God heareth not sinners: but if any man be a worshipper of God, *and doeth his will*, him he heareth." (John 9v31). Yes, and it is also true that He will hear those repentant souls who call upon His name for salvation. (Acts 2v21). Surely those of us who know Him can say with the Psalmist..."If I regard iniquity in my heart, the Lord will not hear me: But verily God hath heard me; he hath attended to the voice of my prayer. Blessed be God, which hath not turned away my prayer, nor His mercy from me." (Psalm 66v18-20). It seemed like an impossible situation; for we had been told that the hostages had been separated, so as to prevent any rescue attempt. "But with God all things are possible!" (Matthew 19v26). "And all things, whatsoever ye shall ask in prayer, believing, ye shall receive." (Matthew 21v22).

Our human minds can scarcely comprehend a situation where a Great Counsellor is always available to hear us (at any time of the day or night) and also hears every other soul who cries out to Him in all parts of the universe - for reasons large and small. He is all seeing, all knowing and all-powerful. "O the depth of the riches both of the wisdom and knowledge of God! How unsearchable are his judgments, and his ways are past finding out!" (Romans 11v33). Also, how precious our prayers are to Him! In Revelation 5v8, we read: "And when he had taken the book, the four beasts and four and twenty elders fell down before the Lamb, having every one of them harps, and golden vials full of odours, *which are the prayers of the saints.*" He desires to hear our prayers and petitions, (Phil. 4v6) so that His perfect peace will rule in our hearts, (Colossians 3v15). We may be gravely concerned about a matter, but our anxiety must never outweigh our faith.

Nowadays when we telephone any department or individual, we are liable to hear the words... "Sorry, we are not able to come to the phone right now, but if you leave your name and number we'll get back to you..." (They might!) Or at other times we may be shoved around from extension to extension, and eventually cut off! The Lord, in contrast to those we may try to contact in the world, is *always and instantly* available. When we know Him, we have a direct line of communication with Him, and we can be assured of answer to prayer - *in His timing.* Also, regardless of *where* we are, He will hear us. On a mountaintop, in a hospital, prison, aircraft, submarine, or from outer space ... that great line of communication is never cut to those who love Him. *Anything* (however small) which is of concern to us - is of concern to Him. Jonah had something major to pray about for he ... "prayed unto the Lord His God out of the fish's belly." (Jonah 2v1), and "at midnight Paul and Silas prayed and sang praises to God: and the prisoners heard them." (Acts 16v25). Sha-drach, Me-shach, and A-bed-ne-go trusted the Lord to deliver them from the fiery furnace. (Daniel 3v19-30). Daniel, himself, that great man of prayer, trusted the Lord to deliver him, although surrounded by lions. (Daniel 6v22). How those answers to our prayers speak to the hearts of the unsaved! After a terribly sleepless night King Darius "arose early in the morning, and went in haste to the den of lions." (Verse 19). He cried: "O Daniel, servant of the living God, is thy God, whom thou servest continually, able to deliver thee from the lions?" (Verse 20) How marvellous was the outcome! The King, on learning of Daniel's miraculous survival, made a decree that "men tremble and fear before the God of Daniel: for he *is* the living God, and stedfast for ever, and his kingdom that which shall not be destroyed, and his dominion shall be even unto the end." (Verse 26) He was the God of these, and many other seemingly impossible situations (too numerous to mention here), and He is the God of equally impossible situations today!

Those who had kidnapped Annetta and her colleagues (thought to be linked to a Taliban splinter group) would surely be ruthless. I had read reports in the past of how members of the Taliban would think nothing of carrying out public executions and amputations in football stadiums. Crowds would flock to see these grisly sights, just as they did during the beheadings of the French Revolution. I felt a special burden to pray that these men (like the lions around Daniel in the den) would not harm their victims, and indeed that they might even feel compassion towards them as fellow human beings.

The weeks of their captivity passed, and each passing day brought horrific news of the continuing war in nearby Iraq. Hostage taking and cold-blooded murder were rampant. A lady of Irish descent, Margaret Hassan, who had worked for the needy people of Iraq all her life, was amongst those who were brutally murdered. The humdrum events of my daily life continued, but I could not erase my mind of Annetta's plight - and nor did I want to. For a while her terrified face could be seen on the covers of Irish and English newspapers throughout the country. Then there appeared to be a 'news blackout,' for the media seemed to be completely silent on the matter. What had happened? Secret negotiations, I felt, were continuing. "Please Lord," I prayed, morning, noon and night, "Free them. Free them all." "Evening, and morning, and at noon, will I pray, and cry aloud: and he shall hear my voice." (Psalm 55v17). Remembrance Sunday came and went, and I thought on the horror of war…

The face of war (like everything else) has changed over the centuries. No longer do knights in shining armour and on horseback, lunge at each other with mighty swords. We have 'moved on' to gunpowder, then dynamite, chemical, biological and germ warfare - and the ultimate in horrors, the nuclear bomb. Never have there been so many on-going 'peace-processes' in the world, in conjunction with so much unrest! … "Peace, peace; when there is no peace." (Jeremiah 8v11). International terrorism, this new phenomenon of the late 20th century, has sadly moved with us into 21st century life. Evil men of the Taliban calibre are not just products of Afghan society. We, in Ireland, have had our fair share of mayhem and terrorism, while crazed suicide bombers are commonplace in the Middle East. Civilians are now targeted as never before, making it difficult for humanitarian organisations to operate effectively. The enemies of democracy are especially the enemies of those vulnerable members of society ... the children, the weak, the elderly, the starving, the poor and disabled. For those who trust in Him, how encouraging are these words in Psalm 60... "Give us help from trouble: for vain is the help of man. Through God we shall do valiantly: for he it is that shall tread down our enemies." (Verses 11&12).

Days and nights of prayer continued as the servants of the Lord brought the hostage situation 'before the throne.' Those prayers, 'that incense' (Psalm 141v2) which is so precious to the Lord arose to Him continually. Then, one memorable day my telephone rang, and a Christian friend of the family told me some joyful news. "Annetta has been released - all three have been released!" he informed me. Because I had not yet heard this news from the media myself, a small doubt remained with me. Like 'doubting' Thomas (John 20v24-29) I wanted to be sure! Eventually, when it was confirmed to me - my joy was complete, and not forgetting to thank the Lord for His goodness (and His patience with me), I felt emotional as I went about my daily chores. Surely the words of Proverbs 25v25 were never more apt ... "As cold waters to a thirsty soul, so is good news from a far country."

The dawn of Tuesday 23rd November 2004, brought that release of Annetta and her colleagues - almost a month after they were taken hostage on Thursday 28th October. The details of the release were vague - probably because no one wanted to jeopardise those who were involved in possible future hostage situations. One of their captors is believed to have been shot dead, but the three victims were safe and well. Only those involved in this traumatic event knew how it was for them, and are able to tell their story. But from the moment that I heard that breaking news, I wanted to tell a story - a story of the great power of our wonderful Saviour, for whom all things are possible, and I wanted that story to have a happy ending. I thank God that it did!

With tears in my eyes, I looked at all types of newspapers on display that week, depicting the smiling face of Annetta as she headed home to be re-united with loved ones. A headline in one Dublin newspaper announced: "Town rejoices as power of prayer brings Annetta home." (Irish Independent, Wednesday 24th November 2004). Even the secular world was acknowledging the power of prayer!

It is interesting to note that during their time in captivity, three Afghan women offered to take the place of the three hostages! What a noble gesture - and yet on hearing of this I was immediately struck by the words of Romans 5v7... "For scarcely for a righteous man will one die: yet peradventure for a good man some would even dare to die." No doubt the Afghan ladies saw the injustice in threatening to kill people who were merely helping with democratic elections. However, who would offer his or her life for someone whom, in his or her view, was evil and even deserved death? Nevertheless we read... "But God commendeth his love towards us, in that, while we were yet sinners, Christ died for us." (Romans 5v8) The righteous Son of God laid down His life for all (1Tim. 2v5&6) in the knowledge that nothing less than this enormous sacrifice could ever redeem the human race.

Valiant soldiers through the ages gave their lives, so that democracy would overcome the tyrants of this world. Annually we remember the dead of two World Wars, and the sacrifices that were made. How much more then, should we acknowledge and honour Jesus, Prince of Peace (Isaiah 9v6) who gave His life for the billions of souls throughout the ages, to redeem them to Himself? I have no doubt that he has spoken to souls through this and other traumatic events, and that He will continue to speak to them in the days that lie ahead - so that they may trust Him for eternity, escaping a worse situation than they have been involved in, upon this earth. "For my thoughts are not your thoughts, neither are your ways my ways, saith the Lord, For as the heavens are higher than the earth, so are my ways higher than your ways, and my thoughts than your thoughts." (Isaiah 55v8&9). A short time after the event, I wrote to a local newspaper wishing the released hostages a full recovery after their horrific ordeal. My letter concluded with the words of Ephesians 3v20&21, which I feel is an apt conclusion to a story that must give God the glory. Perhaps, too, it may have even more joyful implications than we would ever have dreamed possible... "Now unto Him that is able to do exceeding abundantly above all that we ask or think, according to the power that worketh in us, unto Him be glory in the church by Christ Jesus throughout all ages, world without end, Amen."

Morning, noon and night our whispered anxious prayers,
Rose in silent anguish to the throne of He who cares.
Oh blessed Lord, we thank thee now, for thou hast said: "Believe…
For if ye are my servants… ye shall indeed receive!"

"Lest we forget…"
War memorial in the village of Richhill, Co. Armagh.

22

A "Genuine" Experience!
(2Tim. 2v19)

(November 16th - November 30th)

The "Budget," in the Irish Republic, occurs on the run-up to Christmas, and naturally enough most citizens are interested in what the Minister for Finance has in store for them - if anything! Ancient civilizations used the barter system, but nowadays (although 'exchange' or 'freebies' columns exist in free advertising publications) very little is available unless we have the money to buy it. Therefore, in order to conduct most types of transaction, or to live at all, we must use money. Nevertheless, as the Bible rightly says... "For the love of money is the root of all evil: which while some coveted after, they have erred from the faith, and pierced themselves through with many sorrows." (1Tim. 6v10). It is against the background of this verse, that I relate the following events which I experienced just recently...

Replacing the cap on the petrol inlet, I hurried across the greasy damp forecourt and into the well-stocked little shop to pay for my €10 worth of petrol. The lady took the €10 note and held it under a light. Looking up at me wearily that early morning, she yawned, "I'm sorry. I can't accept this. It's counterfeit."

"Really?" I exclaimed. "But it looks perfectly o.k. to me!" She looked at me suspiciously. "I don't think so. This is the second one I've encountered this week, and I've seen plenty more before that, but why don't you check it out with the bank? Their equipment will tell you for certain."

"I'm sorry. I had no idea," I said sheepishly, while rooting for alternative change. I sincerely hoped that she didn't suspect me of fraud!

Stuffing it into a separate compartment of my handbag, I started up the car to a chorus of - "What kept you so long in there Mum?" Next day I was in a large chain store, where I noticed that the assistant was using a marker-type implement to check the incoming notes. "I've been told that this is counterfeit. Could you check it with your equipment?" I asked her, in the faint hope that perhaps it was genuine after all. "Well, it seems o.k. to me," the assistant assured me, after testing it. "However, you would still need to take it to the bank - perhaps our equipment isn't quite as good."

A short time later I was to be found standing in a bank, where my worst suspicions were confirmed. Yes, it felt and looked authentic, but when held up to the light of the bank's excellent equipment, it failed miserably. "Let me show you," explained the helpful cashier - "Look firstly at this real note." I was amazed. A kaleidoscope of intricate shapes and colours as beautiful as the rainbow came to life under the bright light. "It's beautiful," I whispered, my thoughts drifting to a spiritual parallel... Then she took my dubious €10 note. "Nothing," I murmured flatly - "It's just like dull lifeless paper."

"I'm sorry about that," sympathised the cashier, "Unfortunately this is a common occurrence these days - even with smaller amounts. They *look* like the real thing, but when held up to the scrutiny of the best equipment, you can easily see that they are counterfeit." Thanking her, I hurried out unto the street, still clutching my 'piece of paper,' but now I was smiling in the sunshine. I felt emotional as I drove home, thinking of that beautiful and fascinating array of colours that I had had the privilege to see. It didn't matter that I had lost €10 - the Lord was teaching me something through this. I thanked Him, too, for giving me an abhorrence of dishonesty in this area. Should I have passed it on, some innocent party would have suffered in the long run. In every situation it is good to ask ourselves: "would Jesus do this?" I remembered a story from years ago, when a famous painting by one of the great masters was stolen and replaced by a counterfeit. For many years professionals had admired its beauty, and no one had noticed that the painting was a fraud. Only an expert at the top of his field had eventually exposed it!

Today we live in an era of counterfeits. We have 'faux fur,' 'cubic zirconia,' (imitation diamonds), imitation rubies, and other 'precious' stones - and in the sphere of architecture we have plenty of replicas and facades. As the old saying goes: 'All that glitters is not gold!' Of course, the latter are acceptable, providing that the vendor is not trying to make us believe that the object in question *is* authentic! Sadly, 'the counterfeit' in these days is an increasing and very dangerous phenomenon in the spiritual realm. There are many that differ greatly from those individuals who make no profession of faith at all, for deceiving themselves; they deceive others and thereby inhibit the work of the gospel. Confusion abounds, because very often the standard amongst Christians is low. Many nominal Christians use the same terminology as Evangelical Christians, but they have never humbled themselves at the cross, recognising that "all have sinned..." (Romans 5v12). It is good to be aware of how an individual stands spiritually, so that we can pray intelligently and fervently for that person. As Christians, let us ask God for discernment and wisdom, for it is easy to be deceived in these days, passing our 'assumptions' on to others.

Jesus said in Matthew 24v24: "For there shall arise false Christs, and false prophets, and shall shew great signs and wonders; *insomuch that, if it were possible, they shall deceive the very elect.*" Unfortunately many deceivers even stand behind the pulpit and their words certainly appear to contain much truth. Just as counterfeit money has been developed to look more and more authentic, so it is in the spiritual realm. Note that even the large chain store's equipment was not able to tell the difference. But at the bank (which is the highest discerning authority on such matters) that great light revealed all! So it is, when we bring our doubts on such matters to the Lord (who neither wishes us to deceive or to be deceived) that He will show us all things, when we sincerely ask for His guidance.

I believe that there is a two-fold lesson to be learned from this simple episode. Firstly we must make our calling and election sure (2Pet. 1v10). There is only one way to get to heaven, and that is the humble way, when we come to the foot of the cross of our Lord Jesus Christ, acknowledging our sin, and asking for His forgiveness. Whatever our standing in the community, we must experience that humility of admitting to all acquaintances that our previous life has been lived outside of God's grace. Alternatively, we may have had an experience of salvation, but strayed from our 'first love.' Whatever our spiritual standing, there is One whom we cannot deceive, and ultimately we must stand before *Him*, our Judge - not some earthly congregation. In James 2v19 we read... "Thou believest that there is one God; thou doest well; the devils also believe, and tremble." There are so many church-going individuals who believe - but that belief must be accompanied by the act of contrition, and the giving of everything held dear to us into His hands. "Was not Abraham our father justified by works, when he had offered Isaac his son upon the altar?" (James 2v21). Just now, He wants above all, that we do not continue to deceive others, or ourselves - for "if we say that we have no sin, we deceive ourselves, and the truth is not in us." He loves us, and wants nothing in return but our undivided love and obedience. "If we confess our sins, he is faithful and just to forgive us our sins, *and to cleanse us from all unrighteousness."* (1John 1v9).

Ultimately every soul must choose between God and mammon, for we read in Matthew 6v24... "No man can serve two masters: for either he will hate the one, and love the other; or else he will hold to the one, and despise the other. Ye cannot serve God and mammon." This verse leads me to a second thought on the incident of the counterfeit money.

There is a day coming upon this earth, when those that truly know the Lord will not be permitted to either buy or sell. We read of this day in Revelation 13v16-18... "And he causeth all, both small and great, rich and poor, free and bond, to receive a mark in their right hand, or in their foreheads: And that no man might buy or sell, save he that had the mark, or the name of the beast, or the number of his name. Here is wisdom. Let him that hath understanding count the number of the beast, for it is the number of a man; and his number is Six hundred threescore and six." These times may occur in my lifetime or yours, but how shall we cope under such circumstances? Surely we can only trust, as always, in our Friend and loving Saviour to carry us though, for if we are faithful to the end, we shall shortly hear those blessed words... "Well done, thou good and faithful servant: thou hast been faithful over a few things, I will make thee ruler over many things: enter thou into the joy of thy Lord." (Matt. 25v21).

Although we presently conduct our business with it, there is no room for *the love of* money in the life of the Christian. In those last days that are recorded in Revelation, we shall be in absolutely no doubt about those who choose to follow God - and those whose choice is to follow mammon. That old deceiver, the devil, is an expert in the art of counterfeiting - but let us not be deceived by him.

"Beware of false prophets, which come to you in sheep's clothing, but inwardly they are ravening wolves." (Matt. 7v15). "Verily, verily, I say unto you He that entereth not by the door into the sheepfold, but climbeth up some other way, the same is a thief and a robber. But he that entereth in by the door is the shepherd of the sheep. To him the porter openeth; and the sheep hear his voice: and he calleth his own sheep by name, and leadeth them out. And when he putteth forth his own sheep, he goeth before them, and the sheep follow him: for they know his voice. And a stranger will they not follow, but will flee from him: for they know not the voice of strangers." (John 10v1-5).

Just as we bring a dubious note to the great light of the bank, so also we must yield, and expose ourselves to that great Light which judges the thoughts and intents of mankind... "For every one that doeth evil hateth the light, neither cometh to the light, lest his deeds should be reproved. But he that doeth truth cometh to the light, that his deeds may be made manifest, that they are wrought in God." (John 3v20&21). May this Good Shepherd be *your* Good Shepherd, and if you have not already done so, may you come into His fold today. "And other sheep I have which are not of this fold: them also I must bring, and they shall hear my voice; and there shall be one fold, and one shepherd." (John 10v16).

Lord, shine into my heart today,
Thy beaming light, that heavenly ray.
May each secret corner be illumed...
And every dark intent consumed.

Above – While shopping centres like the Stephen's Green Centre in Dublin are on the increase, churches like this one in Co. Meath are no longer used as places of worship – an ominous sign of our times.

23

A Winter's Tale – That Must be Told!
(Matthew 11v28)

(December 1st - December 15th)

I saw her standing there, the little old lady in the confectionery aisle. "I hate Christmas! I hate it!" She spluttered with heartfelt venom. "Where am I going to get the money for all this, with only the pension?" I parked my trolley to sympathise. She looked so worn out, and those clothes of hers had seen better days. "Yes," I agreed with her, "prices *had* gone 'through the roof' since our currency had switched to the Euro." I tried to reassure her. "Don't worry about buying Christmas presents for people. It's the simple things in life that count, and anyway, it was never meant to be like this …" I gestured vaguely at the shelves around us, muttering the usual clichés about commercialisation. How I could understand her weariness and frustration! Pushing the trolley on towards further aisles, I caught little snatches of conversation.

The supermarket, I have discovered, is a minefield of information for the anthropologist. A journey from entrance to exit can be akin to a mini 'Pilgrim's Progress' - especially at Christmas time. Temptation is everywhere, and people are typically at their most stressed and impatient. In fact, from a recent survey I learned that Christmas creates more stress than any other social occasion - apart from preparing for a wedding! Ironically the 'season of goodwill' produces more fatal road accidents; violence in general is on the increase; women's refuge centres are fuller - and the Samaritans are inundated with calls!

The newspapers, placed strategically at the supermarket entrance, proclaim the gloomy shocking headlines … "Pedestrian killed in hit and run. Drink-driver arrested." Or … "Man's nose bitten off in frenzied attack." Magazines show us images of glamour models, depicting how we're supposed to look for the festive season. Housekeeping magazines may make us feel inadequate, as we look at designer furniture and immaculate rooms.

I watch as 'Mr. and Mrs. Rich', a civilised devoted couple and the proud owners of a new Mercedes and fully pedigree pets, hesitate at this section before moving on. She chooses an expensive magazine, and he an up-market financial newspaper. As they move along, he with his eyes scanning the health of his investments, she will inevitably select luxury items, and never 'economy' class, or the supermarket's 'own brand.'

Moving along, I see a veritable mountain of turkey and ham before me. 'Ms. Eco Warrior', a vegetarian and chairperson of the 'Philosophical and Tree Hugging Society' glares at those 'vultures' hovering in this area. (Boy, if looks could kill!) A frustrated mother tries to calm her screaming baby, while simultaneously attempting to mentally calculate which size of turkey would be needed for the two days of feasting, for twenty people. Another mother tries to prevent her mischievous toddler from knocking over everything in sight. He grins up at me, his face an absolute mess of sticky chocolate.

Thinking of chocolate, I smile at the little boy for reminding me that I must get some selection boxes. The 'Pillar of Society' has just marched swiftly into this particular aisle ahead of me. I admire his single-minded determination as he picks out a dozen for his Sunday school class - or is it the Boy Scouts? He proceeds to join the small queue 'for baskets.' He has come in for selection boxes - and he will go out with selection boxes. Nothing else will tempt him. Sometimes I wish that I could be so focussed, but I know that I'll probably always be one of those people who are easily side-tracked!

Sure enough, my eyes are already straying towards something tempting in the 'home-baking' section. Here I notice a humble looking little housewife being lectured in the art of 'organisation,' by an overbearing older lady, with an upper-class accent. Full of the joys of her seasonal skills, she announces to all who will hear that 'she has everything under control.' "Oh, you're only buying the ingredients *now* dear?" she purrs. "I've made my cake and pudding *ages ago* ... back in September actually ..." Sighing heavily (and feeling about 2' shorter) I move my now laden trolley quickly past that particular aisle, narrowly missing 'the party animal,' who has just flown out of a semi-lit area with her small trolley full of alcohol and cigarettes - but no food. Yes, the wine and spirits section is certainly a 'hive' of more activity than usual, with bottles clinking around by the score. And then the nightmare begins…

Dozens of people throng the checkouts. Now, which queue should I join? (I usually make the wrong choice in these situations.) A lady on a mobility scooter smiles up at me. "Awful, isn't it? And it'll be all over in a few days…" She sighs. I nod, in silent agreement. After what seems like an hour (but I'm sure it isn't) of being jostled by struggling, sweating shoppers and screaming toddlers (who've been traumatised in Santa's grotto), and having my ears assaulted by that irritating seasonal jingle, 'I wish it could be Christmas every day,' I eventually stumble towards the cashier. "Well, are you all set for the big day?" Her cheerful voice reaches me through the mêlée. "I suppose so," I mutter vaguely, furiously transferring groceries into the trolley.

Breathing a sigh of relief, I push the heavy shopping trolley towards the exit, but accidentally hit someone. Apologising profusely, I turn away in embarrassment and am immediately confronted by several charity collectors, shaking their tins in unison at me. Behind them an out-of-tune carol is sung heartily by a motley crew. "Come on then, dig deep for the homeless," their spokesman implores loudly. 'Digging deep' for conscience sake (and wondering later about their credentials) I continue my arduous trek up the slope to the car park. 'Miss Power Walker,' an avid gymnast, has just jogged past me with a little trolley full of organic 'rabbit food.' There *is* a lift, but a very unreliable one, as I have discovered on more than one occasion. (That's another story, for another day!) Feeling unwell and a little dizzy, I continue to push the trolley up the steep incline.

Suddenly two large hands grip it from the other side, and I am no longer burdened by that terrible weight bearing down upon me. "That's much too heavy for one person," booms the manly voice. "Oh, thanks a million," I gasp. "I really appreciate your help." However, I discover now, that although my hands are on the trolley, I am no longer pushing it at all. Effortlessly, and in seemingly very little time, he has pulled the trolley up to the car park. I smile gratefully at the departing stranger, who gives an old-fashioned salute as he disappears (as fast as he appeared) into the darkness of the frosty evening.

Gazing at the clear night sky, its stars glittering, and its pale moon reflected on the shining tarmac, I stand quietly for a moment, as if transported to another world. Whispering from time immemorial, I hear a gentle voice touching my weary soul ... "Be still and know that I am God ..." (Psalm 46v10). Overwhelmed by the peace and fresh air and after the turmoil of the supermarket below, with tears in my eyes I thank God for His love to me. I thank Him for sending someone to take my burden away, for I know that all good things come from Him. I wonder, as I look heavenwards, which of those glittering stars so far away in time and space, may have "stood over where the young child was?" (Matt. 2v9). That multitude of shining stars and that great multitude of Abraham's children, the children of faith, who are "as the sand which is by the sea shore innumerable." (Heb. 11v12). Surely I too, as a child of faith, am a "stranger and pilgrim on the earth." (Heb.11v13). I struggle with these, the traditions of my countrymen and women, their times, their feast days, and the things that seemingly 'must be done.' But only in the stillness of His presence, do I find that "peace which passeth all understanding." (Phil. 4v7).

I thank Him for leaving Heaven's glory to dwell in a world of confusion, violence, hunger and disease - and for allowing Himself to be that once-for-all sacrifice for an undeserving human race. How wonderful if each and every one could sing in glorious unity...

"Jesus my Saviour to Bethlehem came,
Born in a manger to sorrow and shame,
Oh, it was wonderful - blest be His name,
Seeking for me, for me!"
(A.N.)

Driving home, my thoughts are full of the characters I have encountered this evening. How I have described them, is the manner in which they appeared to me - and yet I realise that there is so much more to people than our initial impression of them. But how my Lord loves each one of them, not willing that one should be lost. (1Tim. 2v1-6)). My thoughts are interrupted as I stop at traffic lights. Crowds are milling around like swarming ants on an uncertain mission. Many are laden with heavy shopping bags, their faces devoid of fulfilment. It is then that I notice him, the man who stumbles out of a public house, his eyes glazed and a look of misery upon his face. He lurches in front of the car as the lights turn green for me, and I simultaneously swerve to avoid him. I watch in my mirror and am relieved that he makes it safely across the road. 'No no,' I whisper with a frown, 'it was never meant to be like this!'

My thoughts return to the humble manner of my Lord's birth. Most of the people I have witnessed this evening would claim to celebrate this, and yet … "they worship they know not what." (John 4v22). As to the date of His birth, nowhere in scripture is this recorded. However, if the world chooses to celebrate His birth, at this time, and in this way, I will use the occasion to proclaim the Best News this universe has ever known - of His birth, His life, His death (once for all) and His glorious resurrection!

The implications of this are marvellous beyond description. 'Paradise Lost' has the potential to be 'Paradise regained' for those (the "whosoever will": Rev.22v17) that will repent, believe, and trust in Him. And, unlike the innkeeper who turned Joseph and Mary away "because there was no room for them in the inn" (Luke 2v7); there is always room in God's Kingdom for the repentant soul. As heirs, we will receive no less than the Kingdom! We are not directed towards some 'temporary bleak stable,' incomparable with the glowing warmth and comfort of the inn, for … "In my Father's house are many mansions: if it were not so, I would have told you. I go to prepare a place for you." (John 14v2). So long as we live in this, the Day of Grace, the Saviour stands with outstretched hands saying… "Come unto me, all ye that labour and are heavy laden, and I will give you rest. Take my yoke upon you, and learn of me; for I am meek and lowly in heart; and ye shall find rest unto your souls. For my yoke is easy, and my burden is light." (Matt. 11v28-30).

He longs for the little old lady to leave her burdens at His feet, for He will meet her every need. (Luke 12 v28-31). Frustrated mothers and busy housewives and businessmen can find rest and peace in His presence, just as Mary did, as she sat at the feet of Jesus, over 2000 years ago. (Luke 10v38-42). Little children may find it easier to come unto Him, "for of such is the kingdom of heaven." (Matt. 19v14). 'Mr. and Mrs. Rich' would be advised to take seriously the words of Proverbs 11v4: "Riches profit not in the day of wrath: but righteousness delivereth from death." To invest in the 'kingdom', surely renders all other investments null and void! And if the 'organised lady' sees that it is more important to be ready for the 'kingdom to come,' than a traditional feast day, He will make His abode in her humbled heart. (James 4v6). What, then, of the 'pillar of society,' or even the 'Sunday school teacher?' Only the Lord knows his heart, but if his good works do not spring from that essential root 'faith,' then the Lord sees them as nothing but "filthy rags." (Isaiah 64v6). "But without faith it is impossible to please him: for he that cometh to God must believe that he is, and that he is a rewarder of them that diligently seek him." (Hebrews 11v6). Also, we read in Ephesians 2v8&9: "For by grace are ye saved through faith; and that not of yourselves: it is the gift of God: Not of works, lest any man should boast."

With 'works' in mind, I think of Ms. 'Eco Warrior' who loves to protect nature. This is admirable in today's polluted world, but does she "worship and serve the creature more than the Creator?" (Romans 1v25). And then there is the 'party animal.' Even within this category, there are so many complex personalities - from those who are 'social drinkers' to those who are seriously addicted, and candidates for Alcoholics Anonymous. To all the Lord would say: "Wine is a mocker, strong drink is raging: and whosoever is deceived thereby is not wise." (Prov.20v1). There is a joy and contentment to be had in His presence, which far exceeds the temporary dulling of pain and sadness in our lives, with the use of alcohol and drugs. And there is no depths to which the Lord will not reach down to pull a soul from 'life's gutter.' "For the Son of man is come to save that which was lost." (Matt. 18v11) "I am come that they might have life, and that they might have it more abundantly." (John 10v10). To those whose only pleasure is in the world He says: "Therefore be ye also ready: for in such an hour as ye think not the Son of man cometh." (Matt.25v44).

In contrast to those who drink and smoke heavily, I think on those healthy souls (like Miss 'Power Walker') who drink pure water, eat healthily and exercise regularly. Certainly, I believe that it is God's will that we take care of our physical well being. Indeed, Paul tells the Corinthians: "Whether therefore ye eat, or drink, or whatsoever ye do, do all to the glory of God." (1Cor. 10v31).

However, only those who have begun *in faith* can "do all to the glory of God." Leading a clean, healthy life will not, in itself, gain us entry to heaven. As always, repentance and faith in the Lord Jesus Christ must be the basis for every wise course of action we take. It is important to note that in 1Tim. 4v8, Paul assures Timothy that: "...bodily exercise profiteth little: but godliness is profitable unto all things, having promise of the life that now is, and of that which is to come."

Finally, I think of the stranger who pulled my trolley to the car park. There was no indication as to his spiritual condition - for all I know he could have been a true Christian, or even 'an angel in disguise!' But as with the 'pillar of society,' good works alone cannot gain us entry to heaven. In Hebrews 9v13&14 we read: "For if the blood of bulls and of goats, and the ashes of an heifer sprinkling the unclean, sanctifieth to the purifying of the flesh: How much more shall the blood of Christ, who through the eternal Spirit offered himself without spot to God, purge your conscience from dead works to serve the living God?" When we "serve the living God" as Christians, then our faith will be evident *by our works* - surely the natural outcome of our relationship with Him? (James 2v18). In James 2v20 we learn that ... "faith without works is dead" - clearly a significant message for the Christian here.

I think again of that heavy trolley, and how relieved I was when the burden was taken from me. Yes, this was my experience when I gave my heart to the Lord. The burden and fear were gone, although my life continued - but not as before. "Therefore if any man be in Christ, he is a new creature: old things are passed away; behold, all things are become new." (2Cor. 5v17). My hands were on the trolley, but I had trusted another with the burden. Faith is the victory that overcomes the world! (1John 5v4).

Nevertheless, Jesus tells me that "No man, having put his hand to the plough, and looking back, is fit for the kingdom of God." (Luke 9v62). To look back down the slope behind me (to the turmoil I had finished with) would have been disastrous, for I would have lost my balance. "Remember Lot's wife." (Luke 17v32). I kept my hands on the trolley, and my eyes on someone stronger than I who pulled my load onward - until my goal was reached. I recall that sense of refreshing peace in the car park, those stars glistening in the sky, and my happiness that I had reached there. But most of all there was that wonderful sense of my Lord's presence. And to think that heaven will be even better that this!

Driving slowly onward through the winter evening traffic, I am pensive with warm thoughts of home, and loved ones by a flickering log fire. Presently, my attention is drawn to the beauty of Christmas lights reflected on the shining pavements. Then I watch again those shoppers - each one a cherished soul for whom He was born, to die, and rise again - that they might walk "the street of pure gold." (Rev.21v21). Faint strains of a familiar melody carry to me on the cold night air, as the sweet voices of school children sing the final verse of Charles Wesley's carol, "Hark! The Herald Angels Sing..."

> *"Hail, the heaven-born Prince of Peace!*
> *Hail, the Sun of righteousness!*
> *Light and life to all He brings,*
> *Risen with healing in His wings.*
> *Mild, he lays His glory by,*
> *Born that man no more may die,*
> *Born to raise the sons of earth,*
> *Born to give them second birth:"*

If only each precious soul upon life's highway could sing these stirring words "in spirit and in truth." If you have never done so, come to Him now, just as you are, with your sin, your cares and your heaviness of heart, and He will replace them with a gift that is more precious than silver or gold. May you find that "rest unto your soul!" (Matt. 11v29). "For the wages of sin is death; but the gift of God is eternal life through Jesus Christ our Lord." (Romans 6v23). "He that spared not his own Son, but delivered him up for us all, how shall he not with him also freely give us all things?" (Romans 8v32). "Peace I leave with you, my peace give I unto you: not as the world giveth, give I unto you. Let not your heart be troubled, neither let it be afraid." (St. John 14v27). "Now unto him that is able to keep you from falling, and to present you faultless before the presence of his glory with exceeding joy, To the only wise God our Saviour, be glory and majesty, dominion and power, both now and forever." Amen. (Jude v 24&25).

"Robin in Song" – *A Painting by Mrs. M.I. (Ella). Hutchinson.*

24

"Behold I Come as a Thief…"
(Rev. 16v15)

(16th December - 31st December)

In the days preceding the Christmas celebrations of December 2004, it was reported that a record number of people were travelling though Dublin airport. Many were returning home to spend the holidays with loved ones; but possibly even more were travelling out of the country - some on skiing trips and others to sunnier climes. These days many Irish people own holiday homes, not only in the traditional destinations of Southern France and Spain with its islands, but now in Italy, Portugal, Croatia, Greece, Turkey and Bulgaria (to name but a few), and in the long haul destinations of South Africa, the American continent… and South East Asia.

How dramatically life has changed from the days of my great grandfather! In that era, even an annual trip to Dublin from Co. Armagh (either by horse and carriage, or Great Northern Railway) was thought to be a tremendous journey. In those days it was usually a case where one emigrated or stayed within the confines of these islands. Only the very rich, those with prestige or in consulate work, or royalty would possess property in far-flung places. Of course there were intrepid explorers and missionaries like David Livingstone, Mary Slessor, John Paton, Johanna Veenstra and many others, but these were exceptional characters in those days. If someone ventured to Australia or America, there was much sadness and weeping, as the great ship launched out from the harbours of the "Emerald Isle" - leaving troubled waves and broken hearts.

What a heart-rending affair emigration was in those days, for those who were parted from each other knew that they would probably never meet again in this life. It has been estimated that between the years 1847 and 1854 more than 1 million Irish people fled to the U.S.A., many as a result of the potato famine. That tide of new immigrants arriving from all parts of Europe in the 19th and 20th centuries was to be the greatest migration in the history of the world. Sadly, many of these (if they survived the grim journey to these 'shores of hope') would be refused entry. These were the 'diseased,' and disabled (both mentally and physically) who were singled out on the grounds that they would have been 'a burden to the state.' One writer likened the experience to 'the final day of judgement.' How glad I am that His servants have nothing to fear from the *real* Day of Judgement, for it will be welcomed by all who love the Lord, regardless of how they appeared to others as they walked this earth. "And God shall wipe away all tears from their eyes; and there shall be no more death, neither sorrow, neither crying, neither shall there be any more pain: for the former things are passed away." (Rev. 21v4)

Nowadays, thankfully, modes of travel have changed dramatically, and exotic destinations can be reached in a relatively short period of time. I have always enjoyed travelling, but as the years go by that enthusiasm has been mellowed with a little caution on behalf of my family. As regards winter travel, (apart from financial considerations) the weather conditions have probably something to do with it! Only *very* seasoned travellers will enjoy 'cruising' in 100 mile an hour gales, or sitting strapped into a shaky aircraft with a few hundred other petrified souls, packed in like 'sardines.'

This year, as always, we would be at home for the Christmas holidays. Softly falling snow added to the seasonal atmosphere that morning. I enjoyed watching it through the kitchen window, while peeling the Brussels sprouts for the traditional Christmas dinner, my memories dwelling on my childhood. I also viewed with amusement a fearless little robin hopping around on the snowy rims of our cats' dishes, while nearby a handsome wagtail dipped his beak and shook his feathers in the frosty birdbath. There is something strikingly beautiful about pure white snow! I could not help but think of that lovely verse in Isaiah 1v18: "Come now, and let us reason together, saith the Lord: though your sins be as scarlet, they shall be white as snow; though they be red like crimson, they shall be as wool."

The afternoon was cold and outside dusk spread its dark cloak early, as we sat indoors around a roaring log fire. I was preoccupied with a present from my husband - a new short wave radio, with a large aerial extension. As an 'armchair traveller' I could access many fascinating far-away places, without having to brave the elements, although it very much served to remind me of what a spiritually needy world we live in! Those words contained in Luke 24v47 are as relevant as ever for the times we live in... "And that repentance and remission of sins should be preached in his name among all nations, beginning at Jerusalem." Running through the short wave stations, a whole new world opened up to me. I would chance on a Moslem 'call to prayer' somewhere in the Middle East, traditional music from a Greek island, some 'Chinese English speaking' propaganda, how the new member states of the E.C. celebrate Christmas - or a North American radio evangelist... I heard him roaring: "Listen to me, you people. *This is* the last day prophet of God!" (I have learned that many cults are using radio as a means of making new proselytes.) This is certainly a sign of the times we live in, for we read in Matthew 24v11: "And many false prophets shall rise, and shall deceive many." Despite this, for Christians who wish to reach lost souls across the globe - radio is an excellent tool. While it is regarded as a serious crime to bring a Bible or Christian literature into certain countries, Christian broadcasts can penetrate borders, boundaries and sometimes even prisons. "So shall my word be that goeth forth out of my mouth: it shall not return unto me void, but it shall accomplish that which I please, and it shall prosper in the thing whereto I sent it." (Isaiah 55v11).

The following day (known as 'Boxing Day' in Britain and 'St. Stephen's Day' in Ireland) I plugged in my earphones as usual, but this time every station was caught up with some devastating news. Massive earthquakes under the sea in the Indian Ocean region had resulted in ten metre high tidal waves. Twelve countries in all were affected, with thousands of lives, and homes and livelihoods swept away by floods in a very short space of time. The lives of many Europeans (including Irish and British tourists) were also lost. Only weeks later did the awful extent of the 'Tsunami' become evident.

'Tsunami', a Japanese word, originally meant 'a large wave in a harbour', but is now used to describe the most destructive of all waves. Unlike other waves, it is caused by neither the influence of moon or sun - but by a giant disturbance under the sea, which may be either a volcanic eruption or an earthquake (as in this case). As coincidence would have it, my daily reading was in Revelation when this disaster struck. Earthquakes are mentioned more in this final book of the Bible, than in any other, and are very much associated with the end times. Jesus tells us in Matthew 24v7&8: "For nation shall rise against nation, and kingdom against kingdom: and there shall be famines, and pestilences, and earthquakes, in divers places. And these are the beginning of sorrows."

As the terrible story of the Tsunami unfolded, so too did many stories of heroism and fortitude. I read a newspaper report of one young girl, a tourist in the region, who saw and recognised the signs of the Tsunami before it struck. Being a student of geography, she was well read in this particular phenomenon, and knew the tell-tale signs of approaching catastrophe. The result was that she raised the alarm within the little area where she happened to be at the time, and was able to save the lives of at least one hundred people. Surely, we too, as Christians, need to be well read in God's Word? His will for us is that we should know the warning signs that accompany the times we live in, and be prepared to warn those souls around us to "flee from the wrath to come." (Matt. 3v7; Rom. 5v9). I am sure that it took courage for this young girl to shout the warnings to the formidable adults around her. It takes much courage for us also, to visit our nearest neighbours, and warn them of the things that we have gleaned from God's Word. But proclaim it we must, going in His strength, for Jesus tells us: "Whosoever therefore shall confess me before men, him will I confess also before my Father which is in heaven. But whosoever shall deny me before men, him will I also deny before my Father which is in heaven." (Matt. 10v32&33). And in Mark 8v38 we learn that… "Whosoever therefore shall be ashamed of me and my words in this adulterous and sinful generation; of him also shall the Son of man be ashamed, when he cometh in the glory of his Father with the holy angels."

As the months and years of our ageing universe pass, we know from God's Word that there will be more and more earthquakes in 'diverse places.' In the latter times, our earth will suffer the most violent tremors ever experienced in the history of mankind. Those of us in western Europe, to date, have had very little experience of earthquakes, and yet, some day every nation of the world will be affected by that great earthquake mentioned in Rev. 16v18: "And there were voices, and thunders, and lightnings; and there was a great earthquake, such as was not since men were upon the earth, so mighty an earthquake, and so great." In Verse 20 of this chapter we learn that: "...every island fled away, and the mountains were not found."

As I write, I have no idea what the immediate future holds for my country, or its inhabitants as individuals. However, I *do* know that if we are faithful servants (Matt. 24v45&46) of the Lord upon His return, then eternity in Heaven is ours. There is much speculation amongst Christians as to the contents of the Book of Revelation, but surely the most important thing is to be "found of him in peace, without spot, and blameless?" (2Pet. 3v14). To Christians He says: "Little children, let no man deceive you: he that doeth righteousness is righteous, even as he is righteous." (1 John 3v7).

Just as God told Noah to be prepared for the coming flood, we are exhorted to be prepared for "that day and hour" which no man knows. (Matt. 24v36). "Watch therefore: for ye know not what hour your Lord doth come. But know this, that if the goodman of the house had known in what watch the thief would come, he would have watched, and would have not have suffered his house to be broken up." (Matt. 24v42&43).

The Tsunami 'came as a thief.' People were not expecting this sudden dreadful devastation which overtook them. Those masses of people who checked in at Dublin airport during the pre-Christmas rush would have made excellent preparation for their holidays. Perhaps weeks, even months of meticulous planning and anticipation filled their lives. How much more should we anticipate and be prepared for "the coming of the great and dreadful day of the Lord!" (Mal. 4v5). "Behold I come as a thief. Blessed is he that watcheth, and keepeth his garments, lest he walk naked, and they see his shame." (Rev. 16v15).

Another interesting fact which emerged from the Tsunami disaster was that many people were saved by climbing trees - which were evidently very strongly rooted, given that they withstood the floods. This reminds me of the righteous man, referred to in Jeremiah 17v7&8: "Blessed is the man that trusteth in the Lord, and whose hope the Lord is. For he shall be as a tree planted by the waters, and that spreadeth out her roots by the river, and shall not see when heat cometh, but her leaf shall be green; and shall not be careful in the year of drought, neither shall cease from yielding fruit." One young boy spent ten days (without food) in a tree, but was eventually rescued. On hearing this, my thoughts immediately turned to the story of "Zacchaeus" who, because of his small stature, climbed up into a sycamore tree in order to see Jesus. How wonderful that Zacchaeus had that desire in his heart to see Jesus, and that he took the initiative of climbing into the tree! Later that day we learn that salvation came to Zacchaeus. (Luke 19v9). Now as "a son of Abraham," Zacchaeus had access to another tree - "the tree of life," which is mentioned in both Genesis and Revelation.

In Revelation 22v12-14, we read: "And behold, I come quickly; and my reward is with me, to give every man according as his work shall be. I am Alpha and Omega, the beginning and the end, the first and the last. Blessed are they that do his commandments, that they may have right to the tree of life, and may enter in through the gates of the city." That "tree of life" which was denied to mankind (Gen.3v24), because their sin separated them from God, is now accessible through the precious blood of our Lord Jesus Christ. (Heb. 10v14-23).

His desire is that you would come to Him now in repentance, finding refuge in His finished work at Calvary - so that you too may have access to that "tree of life." Remember that the abundant life which Jesus gives is nothing to do with abundance in wealth and possessions. A Tsunami victim who has lost all everything, but has put his trust in the Lord Jesus Christ, is one of the richest people on earth! While this Day of Grace remains, He stands, still knocking at the doors of the hearts of those who know Him not. "Behold I stand at the door, and knock: if any man hear my voice, and open the door, I will come in to him, and will sup with him, and he with me." (Rev.3v20).

To those who know Him, He says: "Behold, I come quickly: hold that fast which thou hast, *that no man take thy crown*." (Rev. 3v11). So long as we are followers of Jesus, and "Walk in the Spirit," (Gal.5v16) this day and all our tomorrows belong to Him. The curse, which came upon the earth because of sin, resulted in many catastrophic changes to our world, but His children need not fear for ... "Who shall separate us from the love of Christ? Shall tribulation, or distress, or persecution, or famine, or nakedness, or peril, or sword? As it is written, For thy sake we are killed all the day long;

we are accounted as sheep for the slaughter. Nay, in all these things we are more than conquerors through him that loved us. For I am persuaded, that neither death, nor life, nor angels, nor principalities, nor powers, nor things present, nor things to come, Nor height, nor depth, nor any other creature, shall be able to separate us from the love of God, which is in Christ Jesus our Lord." (Rom. 8v35-39).

Some day that curse upon our earth shall be removed, and terrible events like Tsunami shall be no more, for we read: "And there shall be no more curse; but the throne of God and of the Lamb shall be in it; and his servants shall serve him: And they shall see his face; and his name shall be in their foreheads. And there shall be no night there; and they need no candle, neither light of the sun; for the Lord God giveth them light: and they shall reign for ever and ever." (Rev. 22v3-5). And so, this life is but for a season, but the years of eternity are indeed "for ever and ever." Without the Lord, those ages of eternity are too awful to contemplate, for we read: "And whosoever was not found in the book of life was cast into the lake of fire." (Rev. 20v15). Why not trust Him for now - and for all eternity? "I Jesus have sent mine angel to testify unto you these things in the churches. I am the root and offspring of David, and the bright and morning star. And the Spirit and the bride say, Come. And let him that is athirst come. And *whosoever will*, let him take the water of life freely." (Rev. 22v16&17). "He which testifieth of these things saith, 'Surely I come quickly,' Amen. Even so, come Lord Jesus." Rev. 22v20). May God bless His precious words to the hearts of all who read, and may "the grace of our Lord Jesus Christ be with you all. Amen." (Rev. 22v21).

Tears of anguish fell so long ago,
With emigration's cruel and bitter flow.
Earthly ties were cut forever,
Loved ones lost to man's endeavour.

Oh that every circle would unbroken be,
On that other shore beyond life's crashing sea,
So find that promised rest, oh troubled soul,
That thy name be called from Jesus' blessed roll.

Dusk falling on a beach along the east coast from Greenore, where many 19th century emigrants to America waved last farewells to Ireland.